CRITICAL DECISIONS

CLARITY IN THE JOURNEY

Connect with God. Connect with Others.
Connect with Life.

Critical Decisions: Clarity in the Journey
Youth Edition Leader Book
© 2006 Serendipity
Reprinted August 2007, May 2008

Published by LifeWay Press®
Nashville, Tennessee

ISBN: 1-5749-4345-6
Item Number: 001314276

Dewey Decimal Classification: 248.83
Subject Headings:
YOUTH \ CHRISTIAN LIFE

Printed in the United States of America

Student Ministry Publishing
LifeWay Church Resources
One LifeWay Plaza
Nashville, TN 37234-0174

We believe that the Bible has God for its author; salvation for its end; and truth, without any mixtu
of error, for its matter and that all Scripture is totally true and trustworthy. The 2000 statement of *T*
Baptist Faith and Message is our doctrinal guideline.

Unless otherwise indicated, all Scripture quotations are taken from the
Holman Christian Standard Bible®. Copyright © 1999, 2000, 2002, 2003 by Holman Bible Publisher
Used by permission.

Scriptures marked NIV are taken from the *Holy Bible, New International Version*, Copyright © 1973,
1978, 1984 by International Bible Society. Used by permission.

13 12 11 10 09 08 07 06   1 2 3 4 5 6 7 8 9 10

CONTENTS

 **EXPERIENCE**

Combine *teaching that engages a large-group* with dynamic *small-group experiences and discussions* and the result is students grappling with reality an real life change. Throughout 13 sessions, small-groups will find power in just bei together in community. Help them connect with God … connect with each other . connect with life! Each session consists of a four-part agenda. In addition, "Get Ready" and "Now What?" segments enable students to dig a little deeper and giv God more opportunity to impact their lives.

 Get Ready

To get the most from this experience, students should spend time with God each day leading up to your session. They simply wrap their brains around the short Bible passages, listen to God, and jot down thoughts and insights.

 So What?

The master-teacher will lead the entir group in understanding what God has to say on the topic. Content has biblic depth, yet is engaging. Students can follow along, jot notes, and respond to questions in their Student Books.

 LifePoint

Welcome and communicate the "LifePoint" or big idea for the session, and then divide students into small groups. NOTE: If feasible, keep the same groups together each week to enhance the depth of group dynamic and potential for life change.

 Do What?

All study should direct us toward acti and life change. The goal in small groups is to be real with each other ir order to connect with God, with others and with life. Students will find powe to integrate truth into life with the su port and prayers of other students.

 Say What?

Small-group facilitators lead students in interactive experiences and discus- sions. "Random Question of the Week" will open students up and encourage them to join activities or discussions that lead into the session topic.

 now What?

To see real power in life, encourage students not to just leave the session and go on with life as normal. The "Now What?" assignments help them continue their journeys and give them opportunity to go deeper with God.

AT A GLANCE

Get Ready

Daily time with God
& your journal

LifePoint

Large Group:
welcome & theme

Say What?

Small Group:
fun & interaction

So What?

Large Group:
teaching & discovery
(Master Teacher)

Do What?

Small Group:
getting real
& connecting

now What?

Continue your journey...

LEADERS AND FACILITATORS

Every Life Connections group must fill three important roles. Each responsibility is vital to the success of the class.

Teacher – The teacher is the key leader of any Life Connections group.

It is the responsibility of the teacher to:

1. enlist facilitators and apprentices.
2. make facilitators and apprentices aware of their roles and be certain these responsibilities are carried out.
3. meet periodically with facilitators to train, encourage, and inspire them.
4. cast vision for and keep the group focused on the goals of the group.
5. guide group members to understand and commit to the group covenant.
6. be sure the group utilizes, fills, and evangelizes through use of the empty chair concept.
7. act as the Master Teacher for the group.
8. keep the group on task throughout each session.

Facilitator – Each subgroup will have a facilitator. It is the responsibility of the facilitators

1. lead each individual in their subgroup to participate in "Say What?" activities.
2. guide those in their subgroup to commit to apply the lessons learned in the "Do What?" section of the weekly session.
3. with sensitivity and wisdom lead their subgroup to support one another during the "Do What?" closing and involve their subgroup in ministry and evangelism.
4. encourage students to go deeper by completing the "Get Ready" and "Now What" sections on their own between sessions.
5. minister to the needs of their subgroup members and lead them to minister to the needs of one another both during and between meetings.

Apprentice – Every subgroup must have an apprentice. When the group consistently has eight or more in attendance, the group should divide into two groups. The apprentice will become the facilitator of the new group and choose an apprentice who will someday be the facilitator of a group. It is the role of the apprentice to:

1. learn from the facilitator of their group.
2. make welcome all new subgroup members.
3. be certain **Student Books** and pens or pencils, and other supplies are available for all students.
4. turn in prayer requests.
5. encourage participation by actively participating themselves.
6. lead the group when the facilitator is unavailable.

CORE VALUES

Community:
God is relational, so He created us to live in relationship with Him and each other. Authentic community involves sharing life together and connecting on many levels with the people in our group.

Group Process:
Developing authentic community requires a step-by-step process. It's a journey of sharing our stories with each other and learning together.

Interactive Bible Study:
God provided the Bible as an instruction manual of life. We need to deepen our understanding of God's Word. People learn and remember more as they wrestle with truth and learn from others. The process of Bible discovery and group interaction will enhance our growth.

Experiential Growth:
The goal of studying the Bible together is not merely a quest for knowledge; this should result in real life change. Beyond solely reading, studying, and dissecting the Bible, being a disciple of Christ involves reunifying knowledge with experience. We do this by bringing our questions to God, opening a dialogue with our hearts (instead of killing our desires), and utilizing other ways to listen to God speak to us (group interaction, nature, art, movies, circumstances, etc.). Experiential growth is always grounded in the Bible as God's primary means of revelation and our ultimate truth-source.

The Power of God:
Our processes and strategies will be ineffective unless we invite and embrace God's presence and power. In order to experience community and growth, Jesus must be the centerpiece of our group experiences and the Holy Spirit must be at work.

Redemptive Community:
Healing best happens within the context of community and in relationship. A key aspect of our spiritual development is seeing ourselves through the eyes of others, sharing our stories, and ultimately being set free from the secrets and the lies we embrace that enslave our souls.

Mission:
God has invited us into a larger story with a great mission. It is a mission that involves setting captives free and healing the broken-hearted (Isaiah 61:1-2). However, we can only join in this mission to the degree that we've let Jesus bind up our wounds and set us free. As a group experiences true redemptive community, other people will be attracted to that group, and through that group to Jesus. We should be alert to inviting others while we maintain (and continue to fill) an "empty chair" in our meetings to remind us of others who need to encounter God and authentic Christian community.

GROUP COVENANT

It is important that your group covenant together, agreeing to live out important group values. Once these values are agreed upon, your group will be on its way t experiencing true Christian community. It's very important that your group discus these values—preferably as you begin this study. The first session would be mos appropriate. (Check the rules to which each member of your group agrees.)

☐ Priority: While you are in this course of study, you give the group meetings priority.

☐ Participation: Everyone is encouraged to participate and no one dominates

☐ Respect: Everyone is given the right to his or her own opinion, and all ques tions are encouraged and respected.

☐ Confidentiality: Anything that is said in the meeting is never repeated outside the meeting without permission. *Note: Church staff may be require by law to report illegal activities.*

☐ Life Change: We will regularly assess our own progress in applying *LifePoi* and encourage one another in our pursuit of becoming more like Christ.

☐ Care and Support: Permission is given to call upon each other at any time especially in times of crisis. The group will provide care for every member.

☐ Accountability: We agree to let the members of the group hold us account- able to the commitments we make in whatever loving ways we decide upo Giving unsolicited advice is not permitted.

☐ Empty Chair: The group is open to welcoming new people at every meeting

☐ Mission: We agree as a group to reach out and invite others to join us.

☐ Ministry: We will encourage one another to volunteer and serve in a minist and to support missions by giving financially and/or personally serving.

Session

1

THE REAL STORY

CoNNecLioNs Prep

MAIN LIFEPOINT: In order to grow into the godly men and women God intends for us to become, we must understand the nature of the world in which we live.

To reinforce the LifePoint, leaders and small-group facilitators should understand the following, more detailed CheckPoints and "Do" Points.

BIBLE STUDY CHECKPOINTS:
· Acknowledge the existence of an unseen spiritual world parallel to the physical world in which we live
· Understand the futility of pursuing worldly values
· Identify three forces that work directly against God's purposes

LIFE CHANGE "DO" POINTS:
· List secular worldly values seen in TV and movies that illustrate the world's influence on our lives
· Develop a monthly spending budget
· Read God's Word daily to better understand our identity in Christ

PREPARATION:
☐ Review the *Leader's Book* for this session and prepare your teaching.
☐ Determine how you will subdivide students into small discussion groups.
☐ Recruit mature students or adults as small-group facilitators. Be sure these facilitators plan to attend.

REQUIRED SUPPLIES:
☐ *Critical Decisions: Clarity in the Journey* leader books for each group facilitator
☐ *Critical Decisions: Clarity in the Journey* student books for each student
☐ Pen or pencil for each student
☐ Three balloons: one filled with air, one with helium, and one with water. Weight down or tie each balloon down to appear the same. Otherwise will make it too easy to distinguish one from another.

Get Ready

Spend a few moments getting to know God. Read one of these brief passages each day, and be sure to write down anything He reveals to you.

MONDAY

Read 1 John 2:15a

Are you a world-lover? What one thing that the world offers could you not live without?

TUESDAY

Read 1 John 2:15b-16

Think about "the world" not as God's creation, but as the systems and ideas that exist but are not of God. These systems and ideas are the schemes of our enemy, Satan. What are some of the distortions used by our enemy?

WEDNESDAY

Read 1 John 2:17

Ever been disappointed by something or someone that you thought you had to have? What did obtaining that individual or thing cost? How did the situation affect your relationship with God?

THURSDAY

Read 1 John 2:24-25

By what standard do you make life decisions? Do you allow Christ to live through you, or do you try to do things your way?

FRIDAY

Read 1 John 2:26-27

Whom do you trust for reliable advice? What role do God's Holy Spirit and Scripture play in helping you make right decisions?

SATURDAY

Read Titus 2:11-14

How eager are you to do "good works" for God? Would those who know you consider you "sensible, righteous, and godly"? When Jesus comes back, where do you think He will find you? What do you think He will find you doing?

SUNDAY

Read 2 Peter 3:10-13

What's your passion? Is it noble? Is it selfish? Describe the kind of person you should be as you wait.

LARGE-GROUP OPENING: et everyone's attention. Make announcements. Open your session with prayer. Read the ifePoint to the students.

 LifePoint

In order to grow into the godly men and women God intends for us to become, we must understand the nature of the world in which we live.

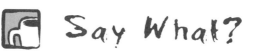

Say What? *(15 MINUTES)*

Random Question of the Week:
Why do the frogs in fairytales turn into princes but never princesses?

Group Experience: Cause and Effect
(Permission is granted to copy only this page for use by facilitators as part of the Life Connections Youth® Critical Decisions study.)

Discuss with students that although we take advantage of many modern conveniences, most of never think about the unseen mechanisms and processes behind them. Use water to illustrate the concept.

Ask a student to explain how water comes out of a faucet. How does it come up to a second story bathroom? How does turning a handle cause water to come out cold instead of hot?

Choose three questions from the following list and ask different students to expla them. Feel free to add to the list, but remember to keep the conversation moving.

How electricity works
Why some people can crack their knuckles
How an airplane flies
How the moon controls the tides
Why we blush when embarrassed
How a flower grows
How a microwave heats food
What causes static electricity
How a computer processes information
How the human brain works

Explain that we take advantage of and personally experience things we cannot explain; therefore, we must acknowledge that there is more to the world we live in than we can see.

LARGE-GROUP TIME:
Have the students turn
to face the front for
this teaching time. Be
sure you can make
eye contact with each
student in the room.
Encourage students
to follow along and
take notes in their
Student Books.

 # So What? *(30 MINUTES)*

Teaching Outline

I. Building a strong spiritual offense
A. Every offense faces an opposing defense
B. The offense must know the strategy of the defense
C. A spiritual defense in the world opposes Christians

II. Learning from the Bible (Scripture)

III. Recognizing the strategies opposed to God
A. Attitudes, perspectives, and values conflict with God's plans for us
B. Worldly messages oppose God and His ways
C. Messages opposing God are not coincidental
D. Some things don't have to be seen to be believed

IV. Defining "the world"
A. "The world" refers to a system designed to turn people against God
B. It makes God's purposes seem unnatural
C. Pursuing worldly values will end in disappointment
D. No one can love God and the world

V. Acknowledging the World's Strategies
A. The "lust of the flesh"
B. The "lust of the eyes"
C. The "pride in one's lifestyle"

Share the "So What?"
teaching with your
students. You may
modify it with your
own perspectives and
teaching needs. Be
sure to highlight the
underlined information,
which gives answers
to the *Student Book*
questions and fill-in-
the-blanks (shown
in your margins).

**TEACHING FOR THE
LARGE GROUP**

Building a Strong Spiritual Offense
In what sport is the goal to get the ball into the end zone and score as many points as possible? Football. The job of a football team's offense is to convert first downs into touchdowns—an easy task if not for the opposition to every play. In each game, 11 defensive players on the opposing team try to prevent the offensive team from moving the ball downfield. Knowing this, coaches prepare teams to fight against a defense by teaching their assistant coaches and players to "read"

1 What makes the offense of some football teams more successful than others?

a team's defense strategy throughout the game. **1** <u>The most successful offense in football are those that recognize the defense's strategies and plan to countera them</u>.

Making a difference for God in this world is seldom easy. Today we will look at the strategies of a spiritual defensive force that opposes God's purposes and God's people.

2 How can you successfully make godly decisions?

2 <u>To be successful in making godly decisions, we must learn to "read" strategie the world uses to defeat us</u>. We must recognize values that conflict with God's Word. By doing so, we will be better equipped to run "plays" that result in victorious Christian living.

So where can we look to gain understanding of the world's defense? The Bible is the best place to start.

Learning from the Bible

Learning from the Bible ...
1 John 2:15-17;
2:24-27

Ask students to read aloud together the parts marked STUDENTS as you read the parts marked LEADER. Everyone should read aloud the sections marked ALL.

[LEADER] ¹⁵ *Do not love the world or the things that belong to the world. If anyone love the world, love for the Father is not in him.*
[STUDENTS] Because everything that belongs to the world—
[LEADER] ¹⁶ *the lust of the flesh, the lust of the eyes, and the pride in one's lifestyle—*
[STUDENTS] is not from the Father, but is from the world.
[LEADER] ¹⁷ *And the world with its lust is passing away,*
[STUDENTS] but the one who does God's will remains forever.
[LEADER] ²⁴ *What you have heard from the beginning must remain in you.*
[STUDENTS] If what you have heard from the beginning remains in you, then you will remain in the Son and in the Father.
[LEADER] ²⁵ *And this is the promise that He Himself made to us:*
[STUDENTS] eternal life.
[LEADER] ²⁶ *I have written these things to you about those who are trying to deceive yo*
[STUDENTS] ²⁷ *The anointing you received from Him remains in you, and you don't need anyone to teach you.*
[LEADER] Instead, His anointing teaches you about all things, and is true and is not a lie just as it has taught you,
[ALL] remain in Him.

Recognizing Worldly Strategies Opposed to God

LARGE-GROUP TIME CONTINUED:
This is the meat of the teaching time. Remind students to follow long and take notes in their *Student Books*.

As you share the "So What?" information with students, make it your own. Use your natural teaching style.

Emphasize <u>underlined information</u> which answers the *Student Book* questions or fill-in-the-blanks (shown in your margins).

Conflicting attitudes, perspectives, and values bombard us. Songs tell you to rage against the authorities trying to control you. Sitcoms show love as sex and depict relationships as being as disposable as last Sunday's paper. The latest movies, fashions, and fads communicate attitudes about morality, money, and relationships. Commercials and other media are all powerful communicators.

Many messages are contrary to God and His ways: a fact that isn't coincidental. An unseen spiritual world parallels the physical world in which we live. Something sinister and sneaky is at work against God's people. And while Scripture is clear that Christ-followers should be on guard against it, many Christians give this unseen struggle little thought or ignore it altogether.

The danger of this approach is revealed in fact. There was a time when no one believed in germs. As a result, many became seriously ill and even died. It was not until the invention of the microscope that physicians could actually see microscopic organisms bombarding human tissue. Only then did they believe in germs; only then did they take their power seriously.

❸ <u>More than ever before, we should realize that just because we can't see something doesn't mean it doesn't exist. Like germs attacking healthy bodies, unseen spiritual forces are daily attacking those who follow Christ. These forces intentionally seek to draw you away from God and His purposes for you.</u>

Defining "the World"

❸ **More than ever before, we should realize that just because we can't see something doesn't mean it <u>doesn't exist</u>. Like germs attacking healthy bodies, <u>unseen spiritual forces</u> are daily attacking those who follow Christ.**

John helps define the Bible's use of "the world." In 1 John 2:15-17, John uses the Greek word *kosmos* for "world." By using *kosmos*, John refers to the world as an order, system, or organization. In the New Testament, *kosmos* describes a system designed to turn people against God. This system reveals itself in the anti-God attitudes and thoughts you encounter at school, at home, and many other places you hang out. When John says "the world," he is not talking about God's creation. He isn't referring to the "amber waves of grain" or "purple mountain majesties." John is not talking about school, work, and friendships. "The world"—as John wants us to understand it—is a system that pulls you away from your relationship with God. "The world" summarizes the often subtle schemes Satan uses to distract us from following God.

The thoughts and attitudes of the world's system are so easy to accept! They often just feel right. In fact, when we choose to live by the world's standards, we often feel more accepted by our peers than when we live as God desires.
❹ <u>Unfortunately, you can be so caught up in the world that living by God's standards seems unnatural.</u>

15

The world promises popularity, power, and happiness if you live by its standards rather than God's. But instead of popularity, the world gives loneliness. Instead of power, the world gives insecurity. Instead of happiness, the world gives pain and emptiness. This is why John warns: "Do not love the world or the things that belon̄ to the world." John does not say, "Don't love people or the things God created." Th̄ "things" John refers to in verse 15 are not the things God made but are things like selfish ambition and pride that can hurt you and your relationship with Him.

❹ How can living by the world's standards affect your determination to live by God's?

Sometimes the things we can't see are more reliable than the things we can. For instance, things ordered from the TV don't always live up to the unbelievable value claimed about them. But some things you can't see are exactly the way the Bible describes them. Take, for example, the *kosmos*. Though you cannot see the scheme of the devil, you can see what happens when people choose to follow him: dreams are broken, relationships end in pain, and spiritual emptiness weighs down hearts

There is an enemy at work among God's people, wreaking havoc on the world and on the people God created. **❺** <u>However, you can live in the world without being controlled by the negative influences found in it.</u>

Acknowledging the World's Strategies

❺ You can live in the world without being <u>controlled</u> by the <u>negative influences</u> found in it.

The Bible teaches us how to avoid living under the world's influences by bringing i̇ dark plans into God's light. In verse 16 John identifies three strategies designed tȯ work directly against God's purposes. He separates "everything that belongs to thė world" (v. 15) into three categories.

❻ 1. <u>The "lust of the flesh"</u> refers to **❼** <u>the internal desires that drive us to seek pleasure with things apart from God. The lusts of the flesh will always consume oṙ thoughts and pull farther and farther into the worldly systems. These compulsions cause us to say things that we shouldn't say, look at things we shouldn't, and waṙ things that we shouldn't want</u>. They cause us to chase after the very things God seeks to save us from, bringing hurt, trouble, and embarrassment.

❻ What are three strategies the world uses to try to pull you away from God and His purposes for you?

<u>Whereas the lust of the flesh tends to originate internally, the</u> **❻** <u>2."lust of the eyes" is triggered more by our environment. Also referred to as "consumerism," thė lust of the eyes refers to</u> **❽** <u>the desire for things we don't need. God provides morė than what we need and allows us to have many of things that we want. Clothes, CDs, electronics, cars, and a weekly allowance are only a few of those things that add to our must-have list. The desire for stuff can get us into a lot of trouble. The "lust of the eyes" can lead to materialism and debt. Relationships can turn ungod̈ as we "eye" a member of the opposite sex with impure thoughts or intentions. It cȧ even lead to pornography addiction.</u>

❼ What is the "lust of the flesh"?

❽ What is the "lust of the eyes"?

❻ 3. The "pride in one's lifestyle" will cause us to develop **❾** a sense of self-worth that is based on what we do and what we have instead of who we are in Christ. This attitude can eventually result in a life of poor self-esteem that affects not only us, but also everyone around us.

John says that these strategies are "not from the Father, but ... from the world." And no matter how good the results of living for the world may seem, they are temporary: "The world with its lust is passing away, but the one who does God's will remains forever" (v. 17). God and His Truth never change. 1 John 5:24 says that, "What you have heard from the beginning must remain in you." If you are able to live according to God's standards instead of the world's, "then you will remain in the Son and in the Father." God can give you victory over the desires of the world(v. 25).

❾ What is "pride in one's lifestyle"?

SMALL-GROUP TIME: Use this time to help students focus on how their lives can be different because of this study as they connect with the other students in the group, the leaders, and with God.

Ask students to divide back into small groups and discuss the "Do What?" questions. Small-group facilitators should lead the discussions and set the model for being open and honest in responding to questions.

Option: Provide three balloons. Fill one with air, one with helium, and one with water. Weight all three balloons down. Invite students to look at each balloon and guess the contents of each. Reveal the contents by allowing a student to breathe in some of the helium and then greet the class. Consider allowing two students to participate in a water balloon toss until it breaks. Make the point that looks can be deceiving.

 # Do What? *(15 MINUTES)*

Group Experience: Looks Can Be Deceiving

Share with students that we generally choose to believe in what we can see, but even that can leave holes in our understanding. Point out that by simply looking at a balloon, you can't tell if it's filled with someone's breath or with helium. Make the point that looks can be deceiving.

1. I struggle with the "lust of the flesh"
   ☐ A bunch
   ☐ Sometimes
   ☐ Hardly ever
   ☐ I'd rather not say

One thing I *feel* distracts me from my relationship with God is

_____.

2. I struggle with the "lust of the eyes"
   ☐ A bunch
   ☐ Sometimes
   ☐ Hardly ever
   ☐ I'd rather not say

One thing I often *see* that distracts me from my relationship with God is _____.

3. I struggle with "pride in (my) lifestyle"
   ☐ A bunch
   ☐ Sometimes
   ☐ Hardly ever
   ☐ I'd rather not say

One area of personal pride that distracts me from my relationship with God is _____.

 # LifePoint Review

Small-group facilitators should reinforce the LifePoint for this session and make sure that the students' questions are invited and addressed honestly.

In order to grow into the godly men and women God intends for us to become, we must understand the nature of the world in which we live.

"Do" Points:

These "Do" Points will help you grab hold of this week's LifePoint. Be open and honest as you answer the questions within your small group.

1. <u>List secular values seen in TV and movies that illustrate the world's influence o</u> <u>our lives.</u> It's not difficult to identify the world's impact on culture when you look for it.
   How can you guard yourself against the negative influences of the media?

Be sure to end your session by asking students to share prayer needs with one another, especially as they relate to issues brought up by today's session.

Encourage students to list prayer needs for others in their books so they can pray for one another during the week. Assign a student coordinator in each small group to gather the group's requests and e-mail them to the group members.

2. <u>Develop a monthly spending budget.</u> Money can be a great asset, or it can get you into trouble. The world says there's never enough. God says, "I want your heart."
How will you invest your finances in such a way as to show your interest in living out God's values instead of the world's?

3. <u>Read God's Word daily to better understand our identity in Christ. Reading the New Testament reveals much about your new life in Christ.</u>
What does the Bible say about how God sees you?

Prayer Connection:

Pray that each of you will be aware of the world's influences and will be spiritually strong in resisting them.

Share prayer needs with the group, especially those related to pulling away from worldly temptations in order to grow closer to God. Your group facilitator will close your time in prayer.

Prayer Needs:

 # now What?

Take it to the next level by completing one of these assignments this week:

Encourage students to dig a little deeper by completing a "Now What?" assignment before the next time you meet. Remind students about the "Get Ready" short, daily Bible readings and related questions at the beginning of Session 2.

Option #1:
Keep a log of the TV you watch this week. List (1) the shows, (2) how much time you spend watching each one, and the (3) values each show presents (parents are silly, love is purely physical, commitment is old fashioned, dirty jokes are acceptable, do unto others whatever you want). How many schemes of the enemy have you identified in what you have viewed this week?

Option #2:
Set up a personal budget. Total all the money you receive each month from employment, chores, and allowance. Then take out ten percent for your church tithe and another small percentage to put in savings. The resulting amount is your discretionary income. Determine what you will do with it.

Bible Reference Notes

Use these notes to deepen your understanding as you study the Bible on your own:

1 John 2:15

love. The Greek word used for love in this verse is *agape*. It describes a love that is unconditional and committed. This is the same kind of love God shows His children.

world. The Greek word John uses here is *kosmos*, and it means that which is alienated from God and is contrary to who God is. It refers to a pagan culture that has abandoned God.

1 John 2:16

cravings. That part of human nature that demands gratification—be it for sexual pleasure, luxury, possessions, expensive food, whatever.

lust of his eyes. Greed that is aroused by sight. A person sees something and wants it. (For examples this see Genesis 3:6; Joshua 7:21; and 2 Samuel 11:2–4.)

boasting. Pride in one's possessions; an attitude of arrogance because one has acquired so much. In its original Greek usage, this word referred to a man who claimed to be important because he had achieved so much when, in fact, he really had done very little.

1 John 2:17

pass away. To give oneself over to the love of the world is foolish because the world with its values and goods is already passing away (1 John 2:8).

lives forever. In contrast to those who live for the moment are those who give themselves to eternal, unchanging realities.

1 John 2:24

See that. John now issues a command. In the face of the lies of the antichrists they are to remain faithful to the Word of God.

what you have heard from the beginning. As an antidote to false teaching, John urges his readers to let the original message that they heard right from the start of their Christian lives control their perspective.

remain. John's point is that when they remain in the truth, they will remain in fellowship with God.

1 John 2:26

lead you astray. Those who left the church were not content to simply form their own fellowship based on their private doctrines. Instead, they actively sought to make converts from among the Christian community.

1 John 2:27

his anointing. The ultimate safeguard against false teaching is the Word of God. This is conveyed to our hearts by the Holy Spirit with whom we have been anointed.

Session

2

THE BATTLE ALONG THE WAY

Connections Prep

MAIN LIFEPOINT: God gives you as a Christian everything needed to battle spiritual forces in the world.

To reinforce the LifePoint, leaders and small-group facilitators should understand the following more detailed CheckPoints and "Do" Points.

BIBLE STUDY CHECKPOINTS:
- Accept that struggles are often spiritual in nature
- Explain the spiritual armor necessary to withstand the devil's attacks
- Understand how to put on the full armor of God

LIFE CHANGE "DO" POINTS:
- Memorize Scripture to help you deal with temptations
- Create new friendships in order to share Christ
- Develop a prayer ministry and faithfully pray for the people God brings into your life

PREPARATION:
☐ Review the *Leader's Book* for the session and prepare your teaching.
☐ Determine how you will subdivide students into small discussion groups.
☐ Recruit mature students or adults as small-group facilitators. Be sure these facilitators plan to attend.
☐ Find a section in the book or cue the audio version of *This Present Darkness* to one of the parts where author Frank Peretti describes unseen spiritual attacks. Be prepared to read or play the excerpt. If planning to read the excerpt, attach a small book light to the book.
☐ Secure a child's set of "spiritual armor" (available at most Christian bookstores). You may choose to use craft materials to create your own breastplate, shield, helmet, and sword. Bring a belt and sandals from home.

REQUIRED SUPPLIES:
☐ *Critical Decisions: Clarity in the Journey* leader book for each group facilitator
☐ *Critical Decisions: Clarity in the Journey* student book for each student
☐ Pen or pencil for each student
☐ Copy of *This Present Darkness* by Frank Peretti (book-on-tape or print version)
☐ CD player
☐ Small attachable book light (unless you are playing the audio book)
☐ set of "spiritual armor"

 **Get Ready**

Spend time getting to know God. Read one of these brief passages each day and spend a few minutes wrapping your brain around it. Be sure to jot down any insights you discover.

MONDAY

Read Ephesians 6:10-11

How have you recently experienced the Lord's strength? In that situation, were you aware of the devil's attempts to interfere in your relationship with God?

TUESDAY

Read Ephesians 6:12-13

Do you ever wonder why there is so much evil in the world? Do you find it difficult resist the temptations the world presents? Describe one challenge you face in dai standing for Christ.

WEDNESDAY

Read Ephesians 6:14

Do you feel that most of what you daily see, hear, and experience reflects God's truth? Picture yourself standing before God. How do your character and conduct measure up to God's standards?

THURSDAY

Read Ephesians 6:15

Do you take the opportunities that God gives you to tell others about Jesus? What prevents you from sharing your faith with others?

FRIDAY

Read Ephesians 6:16

Is your faith based on circumstances or does it consistently grow in spite of them? How do you respond to temptations? Is your faith in Christ strong enough to brush off the empty promises and ultimate discouragement that Satan throws your way?

SATURDAY

Read Ephesians 6:17

Do you ever doubt God's power to carry you through *any* circumstance? How might better understanding and applying Scripture to your life help?

SUNDAY

Read Ephesians 6:18

What do you pray for? Whom do you pray for? When do you pray? In your life, has prayer become a ritual or is it a passionate conversation with your Heavenly Father?

LARGE-GROUP OPENING:
et everyone's attention. Make announcements. Open your session with prayer. Read the ePoint to the students.

Ask students to share bout last week's "Now What?" options. Ask them to brainstorm the worldly values they identified in the TV shows they watched during the week. Ask w they are doing after ing one week on their new monthly budgets.

 ## LifePoint

God gives you as a Christian everything needed to battle spiritual forces in the world.

SMALL-GROUP TIME:
Instruct students to
separate into smaller
groups of 4-8,
preferably in a circle
configuration. Call on
the mature student
or adult leaders you
recruited to facilitate
each small group
through this "Say
What?" segment.

Say What? *(15 MINUTES)*

Random Question of the Week:
What causes knuckles or toes to make that popping sound when you crack them?

Group Experience: "This Present Darkness"
*(Permission is granted to copy only this page for use by small-group
facilitators as part of the Life Connections® Clarity in the Journey study.)*

Ask students to relax either on the floor or in chairs. Darken the room. Tell student
to remain totally silent for the next few minutes, using their imaginations to
picture the action and events they are about to hear. Use the reading light
to read the excerpt from *This Present Darkness*, or cue the audio book.

When you finish, pause. Allow silence to fill the room until a
student speaks. Then ask students to share their reactions
to the reading. You may choose to ask the following:

· How did what you heard make you feel?

· Have you ever read anything like that before? If so, what did you read?

· Did the reading remind you of any movies or TV shows you've seen?

· Why do you think the author wrote about these things?

· What kind of battle does this excerpt describe?

Point out that the excerpt is from Christian author, Frank Peretti's book, *This
Present Darkness*. Tell students that the work is fiction. The characters, places, a
events are not actual people or places. They exist only in the author's imagination

Read Ephesians 6:10-18. Point out the phrase "this darkness." Share that "this
darkness" refers to Satan's constant battle for control over our hearts and minds.

ARGE-GROUP TIME:
Have the students
turn to face the front
for this teaching
time. Be sure you can
make eye contact
with each student in
the room. Encourage
students to follow
along and take notes
in their *Student Books*.

Share the "So What?"
teaching with your
students. You may
modify it to meet
your needs. Be sure
to highlight the
nderlined information,
which gives answers
to the *Student Book*
questions and fill-in-
the-blanks (shown
in your margins).

So What? *(30 MINUTES)*

Teaching Outline

I. Suiting Up
  A. Anything worthwhile takes a great deal of preparation
  B. Some equipment is absolutely essential
  C. God provides all we need to survive in this world

II. Learning from the Bible (Scripture)

III. Acknowledging the Spirit World
  A. The book of Ephesians deals with spiritual insight
  B. God's Spirit is present in every Christian
  C. The spirit of darkness is prevalent in the world

IV. Putting on Spiritual Armor in a Spiritually Dark World
  A. Truth
  B. Righteousness
  C. Readiness to share the gospel
  D. Faith
  E. Assurance of salvation
  F. God's Word
  G. Prayer

Suiting Up

You've dreamed about it all your life. The last several months have been full of intensive training. You adjusted to antigravity. You did not fail to push all the right buttons on the simulated console. You survived several days of cramped quarters. But now it's time: *you* are about to be the first person to investigate an alien planet's surface. When you unlock the door to the outer chamber, you will be only steps away from making history.

Click! The cockpit door opens. You walk through it, unlatch the outer door, and step out of your spacecraft. With a look of wonder on your face, you step to the surface of Planet X. You open your mouth to voice your thoughts, but everything fades to black.

**TEACHING FOR THE
LARGE GROUP**

❶ What makes an
astronaut's helmet
an essential part
of exploring an
alien planet?

❷ Spiritual <u>survival</u>
requires <u>equipment</u> that
only God can supply.

Learning from
the Bible ...

Ephesians 6:10-18

Lucky for you, your fellow astronaut drags you back into the
spacecraft milliseconds before you disintegrate into a gazillion
earthling pieces. As you slowly come to, you wonder what went
wrong. You spent a lifetime dreaming of this day, years in intensive
training, and quadruple-checked every part of the mission.

Confused, you catch your reflection in the mirrored facemask of your
helmet—your helmet that is still on the shelf in your equipment bay!
Horrified, you realize you never put it on. **❶** <u>Without the oxygen supplied
through the mouthpiece in your helmet, it's a wonder you even survived</u>.

Living life without the proper equipment could get you into an eternity of
trouble, too. With food, water and shelter you can certainly physically survive.
However, **❷** <u>spiritual survival requires equipment that only God can supply</u>.

Learning from the Bible

*[10] Finally, be strengthened by the Lord and by His vast strength. [11] Put on the full
armor of God so that you can stand against the tactics of the Devil. [12] For our battle
is not against flesh and blood, but against the rulers, against the authorities, against
the world powers of this darkness, against the spiritual forces of evil in the heavens.
[13] This is why you must take up the full armor of God, so that you may be able to resist
in the evil day, and having prepared everything, to take your stand. [14] Stand, therefore*

> *with truth like a belt around your waist,
> righteousness like armor on your chest,
> [15] and your feet sandaled with readiness
> for the gospel of peace.
> [16] In every situation take the shield of faith,
> and with it you will be able to extinguish
> the flaming arrows of the evil one.
> [17] Take the helmet of salvation,
> and the sword of the Spirit, which is
> God's word.*

*[18] With every prayer and request, pray at all times in the Spirit, and stay
alert in this, with all perseverance and intercession for all the saints.*

LARGE-GROUP TIME
CONTINUED:
This is the meat of the
teaching time. Remind
students to follow
along and take notes in
their *Student Books.*

As you share the
"So What?" information
with students, make
it your own. Use your
natural teaching style.

Emphasize the
underlined information,
which answers the
Student Book questions
or fill-in-the-blanks
(shown in your margins).

❸ What is the theme
of Ephesians?

❹ What two things
does Paul pray the
Christians in Ephesus
will receive?

❺ True or False:
The reason I struggle
with my parents and
friends is because of
my attitude. (False)

Acknowledging the Spirit World

After talking to the Ephesian Christians about relationships
(Eph. 5:22-33; 6:1-9), Paul turns his attention back to the issue
of spiritual insight. **❸** <u>Most of the letter to the Ephesians deals
with spiritual insight and power.</u> Paul leads up to his most direct
acknowledgement of the spiritual battle between Christians and the
powers of the darkness by praying that God will provide readers with
❹ <u>wisdom (1:17) and power (3:16).</u> He warns of returning to the
"dark side" from where Christ had delivered them: "For it is even
shameful even to mention what is done by them in secret" (5:12).

Have you ever been home by yourself, feeling that you aren't
alone or that someone is watching you? Do you ever look in your
rear- view mirror, almost expecting to see two big, red eyes looking
back at you? Have you ever been so creeped out that when you
get to your doorstep you can't seem to get the key in the lock?

The good news is that you really are never alone. God
is always with you and watching over you. His Spirit
is living in you. You can rejoice in that truth.

God has won the battle for your body and your mind. Because
God "renewed your mind" when you became a Christ-follower, you
are to think pure and God-honoring thoughts. But because of the
influences of the world (and those two chili dogs you scarfed down)
sometimes your mind and heart start racing with the fear of the
unknown. Although there is no boogey man, the spiritual darkness
present in the world messes with your mind. It attacks your spirit in
subtle ways that affect you much like imaginary ghosts or ghouls.

Putting on Spiritual Armor in a Spiritually Dark World

With what sounds like both a command and encouragement—"Be
strengthened by the Lord"—Paul talks specifically about how
Christians are to "dress" before going out into the world. In
Ephesians 6:10-18 Paul gives a specific list of garments. His aim
is to show us that we can be equipped to address the inevitable
struggles we'll face as we try to live out God's purposes in this
world. **❺** <u>Paul makes it clear that evil is behind the scenes,
working against your relationship with God and others.</u>
He says to "put on the full armor of God so that you can stand against the
tactics of the Devil" (v. 11). Then he reveals a line of thought straight from a

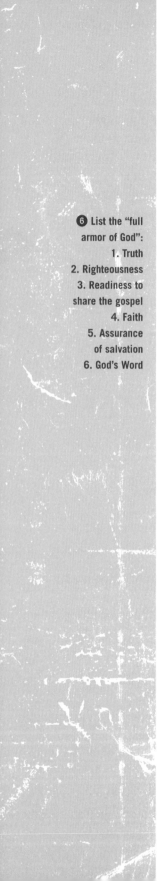

scary movie. But instead of whispering it in fear, Paul shouts in confidence, knowing that the battle has already been won: "Our battle is not against flesh and blood." It's spiritual. We're tempted to think only of what we can see with our physical eyes. But when we look at the world through eyes of faith, we see the spiritual battle that rages around us.

Using the armor and equipment of a first century Roman soldier, Paul says that ❻ truth is to be worn around our waist "like a belt" (v. 14); not coincidentally, that's the first piece of armor a Roman soldier put on. Worn underneath his armor, the belt held his sword—securing his primary offense. Satan's lies seem so convincing that only the truth of God's Word can reveal them. God's Word will help you uncover the enemy's plot to capture your mind and heart.

❻ Paul describes righteousness as a breastplate. In Roman times, chest armor protected the vital organs, including the heart. At the moment of your salvation, God made you righteous. The status given to you by God allows you to stand before Him. When God sees us, He sees the righteousness of Christ. That God-given righteousness is armor that protects our hearts, preventing Satan from effectively attacking our character and identity in Christ. Referring to the footwear of a soldier, ❻ Paul says that your feet should be "sandaled with readiness for the gospel of peace" (v. 15). Soldiers fight to ensure the peace. They go wherever their orders send them. God has sent each of us into the world to share the gospel of Jesus wherever we go. We should have our laces tied and ready to go for God when He calls. An untied shoestring—not being ready—could trip us up. Spending too much time tying our shoes—self-centeredness—is only one way that Satan will use to distract us from telling others about Christ's love for them.

❻ In verse 16, Paul mentions the "shield of faith." A Roman soldier's shield was large enough for him to hide behind. It would catch flying arrows that had been dipped in tar and sat on fire. The "flaming arrows of the evil one" (v. 16) are the temptations and discouragements we face every day. You can trust your faith in God to protect you from everything that the devil throws at you.

❻ List the "full
armor of God":
1. Truth
2. Righteousness
3. Readiness to
share the gospel
4. Faith
5. Assurance
of salvation
6. God's Word

❻ The "helmet of salvation" (v. 17) is a reminder of victory. The soldier wore his helmet not only to protect his head but also to symbolize military victory. The enemy tries to get in our heads, telling us that we are worthless or unimportant in God's kingdom. Through salvation, however, we know that the battle is already over and the victory has ben won by Jesus Christ. We belong to and are loved by Him.

❻ Finally, Paul tells us to take "the sword of the Spirit, which is God's word" (v. 17). The sword is the only offensive weapon in the "full armor of God." But it is enough. Even before you come under attack, you can arm yourself with Scripture to defeat the temptations that you face. Your determination to actively read and memorize Scripture will take the devil by surprise. When you live by Scripture's teachings rather than falling for the devil's lies, Satan will not know what hit him.

Paul tells us that before, during, and after spiritual battle we are to pray. Since the battle for our hearts is never-ending, we are to "stay alert" and never give up praying for each other (v. 18) until we find final victory in Heaven.

 # Do What? *(15 MINUTES)*

Group Experience: Ready for Battle

Secure a child's set of "spiritual armor" (available at most Christian bookstores) or use craft materials to create your own breastplate, shield, helmet, and sword. Bring a belt and sandals from home. Display the armor in a location where all groups can see it.

1. On a scale of one to five (with one being "I have no idea what I'm doing" and five being "I've mastered it"), how well have you mastered the use of each piece of spiritual armor?
   - Belt _____
   - Breastplate _____
   - Sandals _____
   - Shield _____
   - Helmet _____
   - Sword _____

2. Complete the following three statements:

One thing I need to do in order to be ready for the
battle is _____.

One thing I need to stop doing in order to be ready for the
battle is _____.

One thing I need to change in order to be ready for the
battle is _____.

3. Right now my prayer life could be described as
    ☐ Constant
    ☐ Spirit-filled
    ☐ Wishy-washy
    ☐ A valiant effort
    ☐ Nonexistent

Small group facilitators
should reinforce the
LifePoint for this
session and make
sure that the students'
questions are invited
and addressed honestly.

 # LifePoint Review

God gives you as a Christian everything needed to battle spiritual forces in the world.

"Do" Points:

These "Do" Points will help you grab hold of this week's LifePoint. Be open and honest as you answer the questions within your small group.

1. <u>Memorize Scripture to help you deal with the temptations that trouble you most</u>. Jesus used Scripture to combat Satan's 40-day onslaught. God's Word is the on offensive weapon you have.
   What do you need to do in order to increase your Bible study time?

2. <u>Create new friendships in order to share Christ</u>. God chose to reveal Himself to humanity through a relationship with His Son.
   How can you win the right to be heard with a new friend so that you can tell them about your relationship with Jesus?

3. <u>Develop a prayer ministry to help you faithfully pray for the people God brings into your life.</u> Prayer is a powerful and often untapped spiritual resource for many Christians.
   Do you ever forget to pray for others? How can you make prayer a daily priority?

Be sure to end your session by asking dents to share prayer eds with one another, ecially as they relate to issues brought up by today's session.

Prayer Connection:

This is the time to encourage, support, and pray for each other.

Share prayer needs with the group, especially those related to areas in which you struggle—areas that keep you from being all God wants you to be. Your group facilitator will close your time in prayer.

ncourage students to list prayer needs for others in their books so they can pray for ne another during the eek. Assign a student coordinator in each small group to gather the group's requests and e-mail them to the group members.

Prayer Needs:

now What?

Take it to the next level by completing one of these assignments this week:

Encourage students to dig a little deeper by completing a "Now What?" assignment before the next time you meet. Remind students about the "Get Ready" short, daily Bible readings and related questions at the beginning of Session 3.

Option #1:
Get out your current yearbook or borrow one from a friend. Turn the pages, identif ing three students you feel do not have a relationship with Christ. Pray for each student. Then ask God to give you the opportunity to develop a friendship with at least one of them. (When the opportunity rises, make sure to take it!) Ask God to give you the time, place, and words to share.

Option #2:
Set a personal Scripture memorization goal. Choose verses suggested by a daily devotion you are reading, from the notes in your Bible, or ask someone for their favorites. Choose to memorize one verse a day. At the end of the week you will ha memorized seven verses. At the end of the month you will have memorized aroun 30 verses. If you keep it up, by this time next year you will have committed at lea 365 verses to memory!

Bible Reference Notes

Use these notes to deepen your understanding as you study the Bible on your own.

Ephesians 6:10

be strong ... in his mighty power. Paul uses the same three words here as he used in Ephesians 1:19, when he first tried to describe God's indescribable power. In order to wage successful warfare against Satan, the Christian must draw upon God's own power. This is a power outside ourselves from beyond. This is not a natural power generated by the Christian.

Ephesians 6:11

Put on. It is not enough to rely passively on God's power. The Christian must do something. Specifically, he or she must "put on" God's armor.

full armor. Paul uses the Greek term *panoplia* (from which the English word "panoply" comes), which can be understood as the complete catalog of equipment needed by a soldier.

the devil's schemes. Evil does not operate in the light. It lurks in shadows and strikes unexpectedly, with cleverness and subtlety.

Ephesians 6:12

the rulers ... the authorities ... the spiritual forces. By these various titles, Paul names the diverse spiritual forces that rage against humanity. These are intangible spiritual entities whose will is often worked out via concrete historical, economic, political, social, and institutional structures. Part of the call to Christians is to identify the places where these evil powers are at work.

the powers of this dark world. It was no empty boast on Satan's part when, during Jesus' temptations, he claimed to be able to give Him "all the kingdoms of the world" (Matt. 4:8). These "world rulers" have real power, and even though Christ has defeated them, they refuse to concede defeat (though at Christ's second coming they will be forced to do so).

forces of evil. Another characteristic of these supernatural beings is wickedness. They are of the darkness, not of the light.

Ephesians 6:13

the day of evil. Although Paul may have in mind the final day of judgment, the immediate reference is to those special times of pressure and testing that come to all Christians, during which steadfast resistance of evil is required.

stand your ground. This is the second time Paul has spoken about standing fast (see also v. 11). Twice more, he will urge the same thing (vv. 13–14). This is the basic posture of the Christian in the face of evil: resistance. "Standing firm" is a military image. Paul may well have in mind the fighting position of the Roman legions. Fully-equipped soldiers were virtually invulnerable to an enemy onslaught—unless they panicked and broke ranks. As long as they "stood firm" when the enemy attacked, they would prevail in the long run. Most of all, their equipment, as will be seen in verses 14–17, was designed to enable them to "hold the position." This is the key to resisting evil.

Ephesians 6:14-17

All the pieces of armor (except one) are defensive in nature, rather than aggressive in intent. Each piece of armor is used by Paul as a metaphor for what the Christian needs to stand against the dark forces of Satan.

Ephesians 6:15

the belt of truth. This refers to the leather belt on which the Roman soldier hung his sword and by which he secured his tunic and armor (so he would be unimpeded in battle). The "truth" is the inner integrity and sincerity by which the Christian fights evil. Lying and deceit are tactics of the enemy.

the breastplate of righteousness. The breastplate was the major piece of armor for the Roman soldier. Made of metal and leather, it protected his vital organs. "Righteousness" refers to the right standing before God that is the status of the Christian, out of which moral conduct and character emerges.

feet fitted. These are the leather half-boots worn by the Roman legionnaire, with heavy studded soles that enabled him to dig in and resist being pushed out of place.

readiness. This term can be translated as "firmness" or "steadfastness," in which case "the gospel of peace" is understood to provide the solid foundation on which the Christian stands in the fight against evil.

Ephesians 6:16

the shield of faith. The large, oblong shield was constructed of layers of wood on an iron frame which was then covered with linen and hide. When wet, such a shield could absorb "flaming arrows."

flaming arrows. These were pitch-soaked arrows. Their aim was not so much to kill a soldier as to set him aflame and cause him to break rank and create panic.

Ephesians 6:17

the helmet of salvation. This heavy, metal head-covering lined with felt or sponge gave substantial protection to the soldier's head from all but the heaviest axe blow. Salvation is like that—but strong impenetrable. The sure knowledge that one's salvation is secure—that the outcome of the battle is already known—is the ultimate defense against Satan.

sword. A short, stabbing sword used for personal combat. The sword is the only piece of offensive e‹ ment in the armor. The main task of the Christian is to withstand the onslaught of evil powers, not t‹ attack, except in one way—by telling the Word of God in the power of the Spirit.

Ephesians 6:18

pray. Paul does not consider prayer a seventh weapon. Rather, it underlies the whole process of spir‹ warfare.

in the Spirit. The Bible, the Word of God, is the sword of the Spirit. So, too, prayer is guided by the S‹ This is, after all, spiritual warfare.

Session

3

THE MANY FACES OF THE JOURNEY

Connections Prep

MAIN LIFEPOINT:
Healthy relationships that honor God don't seek the approval of the world but rely on the wisdom and peace of God.

To reinforce the LifePoint, leaders and small group facilitators should understand the following more detailed CheckPoints and "Do" Points.

BIBLE STUDY CHECKPOINTS:
· Explain the importance of positively contributing to relationships
· Identify the negative consequences of living by the world's wisdom
· Understand how godly wisdom results in healthy relationships

LIFE CHANGE "DO" POINTS:
· Evaluate your relationship-wisdom according to the six aspects of godly wisdom
· Seek forgiveness from those you have hurt
· Ask God to empower you to be a peacemaker

PREPARATION:
☐ Review the *Leader's Book* for this session and prepare your teaching.
☐ Determine how you will subdivide students into small discussion groups.
☐ Recruit mature students or adults as small-group facilitators. Be sure these facilitators plan to attend.
☐ Provide a blank diary or composition book and pen for each student.

REQUIRED SUPPLIES:
☐ *Critical Decisions: Clarity in the Journey* leader book for each group facilitator
☐ *Critical Decisions: Clarity in the Journey* student book for each student
☐ Pen or pencil for each student
☐ Blank diary or composition book for each student

 Get Ready

Spend a few moments getting to know God. Read one of these brief passages each day, and be sure to write down anything He reveals to you.

MONDAY

Read James 3:13

Do your friends come to you when experiencing relationship problems? Do you se to understand the problems they bring?

TUESDAY

Read James 3:14

When did you last do something for someone other than yourself? When did you c ebrate—without any thought for you—because of something good that happene to someone else?

WEDNESDAY

Read James 3:15

Do your attempts to make things better ever make the original problem worse? D you give your opinion on a subject before anyone asks your advice?

THURSDAY

Read James 3:16

Would you say that you are wise or just a wise guy? When you consider your relationships, do most of them seem easy-going or full of conflict and unresolved problems?

FRIDAY

Read James 3:17

What adjectives would those who know you best use to describe the kind of friend you are? Could the words *gentle* and *merciful* be used to describe how you treat others?

SATURDAY

Read James 3:17

Are the motivations for your relationships pure or are you always thinking about how you can benefit from them? Do you treat some people differently than others? How would you feel if someone called you a hypocrite?

3

SUNDAY

Read James 3:18

Are relationships easy for you or difficult? Would you consider yourself a peace-maker? If so, explain.

E-GROUP OPENING:
t everyone's attention.
announcements. Open
session with a prayer.
ad the LifePoint to the
students.

sk students about last
week's "Now What?"
ns. Ask them to share
the progress they are
aking in building new
lationships in order to
share Christ. Ask for a
lunteer to share some
he Scripture he or she
memorized. Recognize
who have memorized
erse every day during
the past week.

LifePoint

Healthy relationships that honor God don't seek the approval of "the world" but rely on the wisdom and peace of God.

SMALL-GROUP TIME:
Instruct students to separate into smaller groups of 4-8, preferably in a circle configuration. Call on the mature student or adult leaders you recruited to facilitate each small group through this "Say What?" segment.

Say What? *(15 MINUTES)*

Random Question of the Week:
What if "dog" was spelled C-A-T? Would it change anything?

Group Experience: Things in Common

(Permission is granted to copy only this page for use by facilitators as part of the Life Connections® Youth Clarity in the Journey study.)

Fill in the following without letting anyone know what you are writing. If you don't have an answer for one of the questions, leave it blank.

My favorite food is_____

My favorite movie is_____

The best place to take a family vacation is_____

If I could play only one sport it would be_____

The most important meal of the day for me is_____

I get nervous when I_____

I study better when_____

The best pet is a_____

Family is_____

Someday I hope to make a difference in the world by_____

Read aloud the first part of each statement as students share their responses. Each time more than one person gives a similar response, indicate that they have something in common. After students complete the last statement, point out those students who seemed to have the most in common. If appropriate, comment on the existing friendship that indicates similar interests or the surprising compatibility that has been revealed. Share that relationships—family, friends, and acquaintances—are gifts from God.

 So What? *(30 MINUTES)*

Teaching Outline

I. Pick Me! Pick Me!
A. Everyone wants to be loved

B. Some people go to great lengths to find acceptance

C. God provides all we need to survive in this world

II. Learning from the Bible (Scripture)

3

III. The Choice Is Yours
A. Everything you do affects others

B. What you sow is what you reap

C. Wisdom is a lifestyle

IV. Six Ways to Bring the "Wisdom from Above" Down to Earth
A. Be a person of integrity

B. Handle anger appropriately

C. Respond to others' feelings

D. Be open to other opinions and ideas

E. Show God's mercy regardless of how you are treated

F. Treat everyone equally and be honest in your relationships

**TEACHING FOR THE
LARGE GROUP**

Pick Me! Pick Me!

These words may bring to mind a certain cartoon donkey, but they are also the cry of almost everyone you'll ever meet. Everyone wants to be picked or chosen for something. Consider th new kid at school. Her strengths are unknown in the early going. It may take some time bef anyone knows what she brings to the table as a friend, writer, or artist; but in time she'll shine. Before you know it, she's the top pick for group-work partner.

God is a big fan of boundaries, too. ❶ <u>Everyone wants to belong.</u> You might not b comfortable admitting it in front of your friends, but the truth is that you need to loved. Why? Because God is love. He created you to love and to be loved. In fact, need for love is so strong that sometimes we'll go to great lengths to experience i

❶ **What one thing
does everyone want?**

Our search for love shows in our relationships. According to James, the brother of Jesu there are two ways to begin relationships. Both involve wisdom. ❷ <u>James tells us that</u> <u>we can build our relationships with either earthly or heavenly wisdom.</u> Our ability to make wise decisions in relationships is directly related to the approach we take. You might think, *School wouldn't be so bad if it weren't for the classes.* Similarly, some people think life wouldn't be so bad if it weren't for the people. Your home, school, tea job, church, and even dreams are packed full of people. If you like them, things are great. But when you don't, things can quickly become frustrating.

❷ **With what two types
of wisdom can people
build relationships?**
1. Earthly
2. Heavenly

Many of the problems in the world today can be attributed to relationships gone sour. Strong personalities, personality conflicts, and strained relationships can make life miserable. You may be miserable, or you may *be* the misery. Either way, you can benefit from a look at what the Bible has to say about relationships.

Learning from the Bible

**Learning from
the Bible ...
James 3:13-18**

**Ask a volunteer to read
the part of STUDENT
while you read the
part of LEADER. Have
the remaining students
read the ALL part.**

[LEADER] ¹³ *Who is wise and understanding among you?*

[STUDENT] I am!

[ALL] He should show his works by good conduct with wisdom's gentleness.

[STUDENT] My bad!

[ALL] ¹⁴ *But if you have bitter envy and selfish ambition in your heart, don't brag and lie in defiance of the truth.*

[LEADER] ¹⁵ *Such wisdom does not come down from above, but is earthly, sensual, demonic.*

[ALL] ¹⁶ *For where envy and selfish ambition exist, there is disorder and every kind of evil.*

[LEADER] ¹⁷ *But the wisdom from above is first pure, then peace-loving, gentle, compli-ant, full of mercy and good fruits, without favoritism and hypocrisy.*

[ALL] ¹⁸ *And the fruit of righteousness is sown in peace by those who make peace.*

[STUDENT] Peace!

The Choice Is Yours

Every day you make your own decisions, but you never make them alone. You make them under the influence of either "the world" or God. That means the relationship choices you make are either good or bad. ❸ <u>Everything you say or do—or don't say or don't do—impacts others both positively or negatively.</u> You may think that if you treat someone like dirt you can still enjoy a happy relationship with him or her. The truth is that even if the other person is extremely forgiving, it will be difficult for the relationship to be where God wants it to be because of how you mistreated a "friend." Paul warns in Galatians 6:7-8 that what you sow is exactly what you will reap. In other words, if you are a good friend you will enjoy good friendships. If, however, you are a bad friend you'll have rotten relationships. That's why we must take care to base our actions towards others on godly instead of "earthly" wisdom.

James defines wisdom this way: it's who you are and what you do. If you want to be wise and understanding, act and speak in such a way as to reflect it. Your wisdom will be evident in your conduct. ❹ <u>4 James describes godly wisdom as gentle (v.13). Wisdom is not knowledge or intelligence. Wisdom is a lifestyle.</u> It shines through your character and the way you get along with others, ultimately proving your relationship with God.

Six Ways to Bring the "Wisdom from Above" Down to Earth

Have you ever heard anyone say, "She's so fake" or "Your church is full of fakes"? This conclusion, unfortunately often based on conclusions perceived as fact, leads to an important point. God would have you be a person of integrity. Integrity is similar to love: it's much more difficult to define than it is to demonstrate. A person of integrity does not lie, cheat, or use people. Those who have integrity don't worry about what they say or how they act because they are people of their word. They recognize that ❺ <u>(1)"wisdom from above" is pure (v. 17)—authentic. The efforts they invest into relationships are real.</u>

❻ <u>A person without integrity takes; a person with integrity gives. A person without integrity is always looking out for number one; a person with integrity looks out for the interests of others.</u> The greatest relationships are built on integrity. These are wise relationships.

❺ <u>(2) The second way to demonstrate godly wisdom is to effectively deal with anger. Why? Because</u> wisdom is "peace-loving" (v. 17).
Are you a hot head? Do you get mad when others don't see things your way? Do you use the silent treatment to manipulate others? Maybe you know the person who is always looking for a fight. When is the last time you were riding with the guy who blows up at every driver on the road? Proverbs 14:29 distinguishes between the understanding of the patient man and the foolishness of the quick-tempered one.

LARGE-GROUP TIME CONTINUED:
This is the meat of the teaching time. Remind students to follow along and take notes in their *Student Books*.

As you share the "So What?" information with students, make it your own. Use your natural teaching style.

Emphasize <u>underlined formation</u>, which gives key points, answers to the *Student Book* questions or fill-in-the-blanks in the (shown in your margins).

❸ Everything I Say or Do Affects Others …
Positively
Negatively
Neither positively nor negatively
Both positively and negatively

❹ True or False: According to James, wisdom is knowledge. (False)

❺ List the six aspects of godly wisdom James 3:17 mentions.

❻ A person without integrity takes; a person with integrity <u>gives</u>. A person without integrity is always looking out for number one; a person with integrity looks out for the <u>interests</u> of <u>others</u>.

Anger is not bad in itself. Anger at the schemes of the enemy is appropriate. Anger that motivates you to do right is honorable. The lesson in these cases is control. But anger that hurts others or places you in a position above someone else does not honor God. The way you handle your anger or angry situations is key to handling relationships with wisdom.

5 (3)The third way to show godly wisdom becomes evident through our gentle or sensitive responses. Twice in five verses James mentions that wisdom is "gentle" (vv. 13,17). To be gentle means to be considerate, courteous, and sensitive to others. To be considerate of others' feelings is not only right, it is the wise thing to do. Being courteous has become an almost-forgotten art. Showing even the smallest common courtesy is another sign that you are wise in your relationships. Someone may have accused you of being too sensitive. If we hear this enough we may start believing it and choose to keep our hearts locked away. That isn't healthy. In too many cases people are desensitized to those around them. The truth is that ignoring or discounting someone else's feelings can crush his spirits. Another proverb says that a healing tongue is a "tree of life, but the devious tongue breaks the spirit" (see Prov. 15:4).

5 (4) When we approach relationships with wisdom, we are open to the ideas and opinions of others. This is the fourth way God's wisdom flows through us. James uses the word "compliant" to describe a submissive attitude toward others (v.17). The wise person is not always the person who does all the talking and makes all the decisions. Proverbs 12:15 warns that if you don't want to be a fool, you are wise to listen to advice.

5 (5) The fifth way to show godly wisdom is by sharing God's mercy regardless of the way you are treated. What is your first reaction to someone who says something behind your back or trashes you to your face? If you're the strong silent type, you may not say anything. If you don't mind telling others what you think, you may start a smear campaign of your own. But Proverbs 17:9 says, "Whoever conceals an offense promotes love, but whoever gossips about it separates friends." **7** Having mercy means that you give someone what they need, not what they deserve. The wise thing to do is to show others God's mercy regardless of the way they treat you.

5 (6) The sixth way to show godly wisdom is to treat everyone equally—striving to be totally honest and fair in your relationships. Are you impartial and sincere in your treatment of others? Or do you show favorites? If you do, be aware that **8** hypocrisy is one reason why some people stop coming to church. Commit to treating everyone as you would like to be treated, no matter where you are or whom you are with.

5 List the six aspects of godly wisdom James 3:17 mentions.

7 Having mercy means that you give someone what they <u>need</u>, not what they <u>deserve.</u>

8 True or False: Hypocrisy is one reason some people stop coming to church. (True)

James says, "the fruit of righteousness is sown in peace by those who make peace" (v. 18). If you are committed to forming relationships based on God's wisdom, your motivations must be pure, not selfish. You must approach people with mercy, forgiving them even when they hurt you. Your attitude toward others must be open and inviting, your actions gentle and sincere. Through these things, you will sow peace in your relationships.

3

SMALL-GROUP TIME:
Use this time to help students begin to integrate the truth they've learned into their lives while they connect with the other students in the group, the leaders, and with God.

Ask students to divide back into small groups and discuss the "Do What?" questions. Small-group facilitators should lead the discussions and set the model for being open and honest in responding to questions.

 # Do What? *(15 MINUTES)*

Group Experience: Wise in Relationships

1. Which of the following best describes your relationship- wisdom?
   - ☐ I've got godly wisdom down to a science.
   - ☐ I try to act according to God's wisdom.
   - ☐ Sometimes I rely on God's wisdom, and sometimes I choose the world's.
   - ☐ I'm worldly wise; I know I need to work on changing that.

2. Which of the following describe you? You may mark as many as are appropriate.
   - ☐ I am a person of integrity.
   - ☐ I handle anger appropriately.
   - ☐ I care about others' feelings.
   - ☐ I am open to other opinions and ideas.
   - ☐ I try to show God's mercy regardless of how I am treated.
   - ☐ I treat everyone the same.
   - ☐ I am honest in my relationships.

3. In order to be a peacemaker in the relationships in which God places me, I will ...

LifePoint Review

Healthy relationships that honor God don't seek the approval of the world but rely on the wisdom and peace of God.

"Do" Points:

These "Do" Points will help you grab hold of this week's LifePoint. Be open and honest as you answer the questions within your small group.

1. <u>Evaluate your relationship-wisdom according to the six aspects of godly wisdom</u> There is no better place to find help for your relationships than in the Bible. **What do you need to do to become wiser in your relationships?**

2. <u>Seek forgiveness from those you have hurt.</u> No relationship that has experienced a wrong can be made right until forgiveness is offered and accepted. **Has anyone hurt you? Whom do you need to forgive? Whom have you hurt? From whom do you need to ask forgiveness?**

3. <u>Ask God to empower you to be a peacemaker.</u> Everything you say or do either creates strife or brings peace. **Pray that God will speak through your words and actions to bring peace into your relationships.**

Prayer Connection:

This is the time to encourage, support, and pray for each other.

Share prayer needs with the group, especially those related to changes you could make so that your relationships will reflect godly wisdom. Your group facilitator will close your time in prayer.

Prayer Needs:

 # now What?

Take it to the next level by completing one of these assignments this week:

Encourage students to dig a little deeper by completing a "Now What?" assignment before the next time you meet. Remind students about the "Get Ready" short daily Bible readings and related questions at the beginning of Session 4.

Option #1:

Ask a mature, Christian friend to be honest about what type of friend you are. Ask them to answer the following questions about your friendship style:

Am I a person of integrity?

Do I handle anger appropriately?

Do I care about others' feelings?

Am I open to other opinions and ideas?

Do I try to show God's mercy regardless of how I am treated?

Do I treat everyone the same?

Do not comment on anything your friend shares with you, and don't get your feelings hurt. Simply take notes on what you're told. Prayerfully consider your friend's observations. Make a point to improve your relationships. This week, take at least one practical step to moving toward the person whom God has designed you to be.

Option #2:

Meet your closest friends for breakfast, lunch, or coffee. Discuss how your friendships are reflecting God's wisdom. Evaluate the inclusive or exclusive nature of your relationships. Discuss how God can use your friendship with each other to point others to Christ.

3

Bible Reference notes

Use these notes to deepen your understanding as you study the Bible on your own:

James 3:13

by his good life, by deeds. Understanding, like faith, is shown by how one lives. Specifically, understanding is demonstrated by a good life and by good deeds. This is what Jesus taught—and lived (se Matt. 7:15–23).

James 3:14

bitter envy. The word translated "bitter" is the same word that was used in verse 12 to describe brac ish water unfit for human consumption. It is not applied to zeal (the word translated "envy" is literall *zelos*). Zeal that has gone astray becomes jealousy.

selfish ambition. The word translated here as "selfish ambition" originally meant "those who can be hired to do spinning." Then it came to mean "those who work for pay." It later came to mean "those w work only for what they get out of it" and it was applied to those who sought political office merely fo personal gain.

in your hearts. This is the issue: What lies at the core of the person's being?

do not boast about it or deny the truth. Those whose hearts are filled with this sense of rivalry and party spirit should not pretend they are speaking God's wisdom. That merely compounds the wrong.

James 3:15

James uses three terms—each of which is less desirable than the previous one—to describe the true origin of this "non-wisdom." There is "earthly" wisdom that arises out of this world. There is "unspiri al" wisdom that arises out of the "soul" of the person. Neither form of wisdom is necessarily bad, exc when it claims to originate with the Spirit of God or violates biblical principles. And then there is wisc "of the devil" that is not neutral. This is literally, "demon-like"; i.e., that which is possessed even by demons (see James 2:19) or is under the control of evil spirits.

James 3:16-18

James contrasts the lifestyle that emerges from pretend wisdom (v. 16) with that which arises out of true wisdom (vv. 17–18).

James 3:17

pure. The Greek word describes a moral purity.

peace-loving. This is the opposite of envy and ambition. True wisdom produces right relationships between people, which is the root idea behind the word peace when it is used in the New Testament.

considerate. This is a very difficult word to translate into English. It has the sense of that "which ste in to correct things when the law itself has become unjust" as Aristotle put it.

submissive. True wisdom is willing to listen, learn, and then yield when persuaded.

full of mercy and good fruit. True wisdom reaches out to the unfortunate in practical ways, a point James never tires of making.

impartial. Literally, "undivided"; that is, true wisdom does not vacillate back and forth. It is the oppos of the wavering person in James 1:6–8.

sincere. True wisdom does not act or pretend. It is honest and genuine.

James 3:18

Peace flows from true wisdom in contrast to the sort of harsh insistence on "truth" that divides peopl Those who sow peace reap right actions.

Session

4

FINDING CLARITY

Connections Prep

MAIN LIFEPOINT: Some of the greatest moments in your relationship with God are those when you stop thinking about you, choosing instead to let your mind and body rest in time spent alone with Him.

To reinforce the LifePoint, leaders and small-group facilitators should understand the following more detailed CheckPoints and "Do" Points.

BIBLE STUDY CHECKPOINTS:
- Explain what it means to "take delight in the Lord"
- Define "waiting on God"
- Acknowledge the importance of depending on God, even after He fills our deepest desires

LIFE CHANGE "DO" POINTS:
- Prioritize your passions according to God's standards
- Be faithful to do the little things while waiting for bigger things to come
- Tell others about how God gives you your heart's desires

PREPARATION:
- ☐ Review the *Leader's Book* for this session and prepare your teaching.
- ☐ Determine how you will subdivide students into small discussion groups.
- ☐ Recruit mature students or adults as small-group facilitators. Be sure these facilitators plan to attend.
- ☐ Come to the session wearing a wristwatch with a second hand.

REQUIRED SUPPLIES:
- ☐ *Critical Decisions: Clarity in the Journey* leader book for each group facilitator
- ☐ *Critical Decisions: Clarity in the Journey* student book for each student
- ☐ Pen or pencil for each student
- ☐ Wristwatch with a second hand

This "Get Ready" section is primarily for the students, but leaders & facilitators will benefit from these devotionals as well.

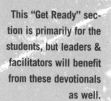  Get Ready

Spend a few moments getting to know God. Read one of these brief passag
each day, and be sure to write down anything He reveals to you.

MONDAY

Read Psalm 37:3

Whom do you most trust? Does the relationship you have with that individual hel
you to be a better person? Explain.

TUESDAY

Read Psalm 37:4

When is the last time you used the word *delightful*? Would *delightful* honestly
describe your relationship with God? If not, what word would?

WEDNESDAY

Read Psalm 37:4

What do you most want in life? What is your heart's desire? If God gave you your
heart's desire, would you be delighted?

THURSDAY

Read Psalm 37:5-6

Do you find it difficult to remain committed to something? What keeps you from
making a commitment? In what ways does God honor your commitment to Him?

FRIDAY

Read Psalm 37:7

What do you expect from God? Is what you expect worth the wait? How patient are you when waiting for God to answer your prayers?

SATURDAY

Read Psalm 37:8

How do you feel when something good happens to someone else? Are you usually happy, or does it bug you that something good has happened to someone else?

SUNDAY

Read Psalm 37:9

What are your hopes and dreams for the future? Do you ever get sidetracked from the plans God has for you because those around you seem to be having a great time without God?

 LifePoint

Some of the greatest moments in your relationship with God are those when you stop thinking about you, choosing instead to let your mind and body rest in time spent alone with Him.

SMALL-GROUP TIME:
Instruct students to separate into smaller groups of 4-8, preferably in a circle configuration. Call on the mature student or adult leaders you recruited to facilitate each small group through this "Say What?" segment.

Say What? *(15 MINUTES)*

Random Question of the Week:

What is the difference between a toadstool and a mushroom? And if you were two inches tall, which would you choose as shelter?

Group Experience: Just a Minute

This activity will demonstrate what it looks like to be obsessed with time. Althoug there are several ways to accomplish this, here is one. Not shouting, but so everyone can hear you say, "Just a minute." As soon as you say it, start looking at your watch. Without commenting, keep looking at it for exactly 60 seconds. If a studen asks you a question, hold up your hand as if to say, "Just a minute." Do not speak or look up. Keep your focus on the time. At the conclusion of 60 seconds say, "Now where were we?" Allow students to respond to your over-attentiveness to the time.

1. How do you feel when you have to wait on something or someone?

2. Where do you most often have to wait?
   - ☐ Doctor's office
   - ☐ Bus stop
   - ☐ In traffic
   - ☐ Online
   - ☐ At lunch
   - ☐ Other _____

3. What kind of "waiter" are you?

☐ Clock-watcher	☐ Hand-wringer
☐ Leg-bouncer	☐ Floor-pacer
☐ Nail-biter	☐ Contented-sitter
☐ Eye-roller	☐ "Fall-asleeper"

4. For whom would you most willingly wait? Number the following from 1 to 10. (1 being the person to whom you would extend the most patience and 10 being the person who would have you scowling at the clock.)

__ Professional athlete   __ Friend

__ Coach   __ School principal

__ Sibling   __ Favorite relative

__ God   __ Boyfriend/Girlfriend

__ Parent   __ Medical professional

ARGE-GROUP TIME:
Have the students turn
face the front for this
eaching time. Be sure
ou can make eye con-
tact with each student
a the room. Encourage
students to follow
ong and take notes in
their *Student Books*.

So What? *(30 MINUTES)*

q

Teaching Outline

I. It's Not Fair!
    A. "It's not fair!" is a universal cry

    B. From almost the beginning of creation, "fairness" has been an issue

    C. Sometimes fairness hurts

II. Learning from the Bible (Scripture)

III. The Good, the Bad, and the Impatient
    A. Godly people worry about the injustice they see

    B. Good things seem to happen to bad people

    C. Patiently waiting for God's justice to prevail is a virtue

IV. Worth the Wait
    A. God will change your attitude so you can focus on Him

    B. Satisfaction comes in spending time with God

    C. God will give you the desires of your heart

    D. Waiting on God is time well spent

    E. Worrying will eventually get you down

TEACHING FOR THE LARGE GROUP:
Share the "So What?" teaching with your students. You may modify it to meet your needs.

Be sure to highlight the underlined information, which gives answers to the *Student Book* questions and fill-in-the-blanks (shown in your margins).

It's Not Fair!

Children learn to say it at an early age. Teenagers fume over the issue, and discuss it with their friends at length. Adults seldom say it, but still feel and respond to it ❶ The phrase, "It's not fair!" has been proclaimed since the beginning of time. In fact, you can easily imagine Adam saying to Eve on their way out of Eden: "It's not fair! We had a good thing going. What we did couldn't have been *that* bad."

For generations, people—including God's people–have wandered the crazy maze called life. And every so often—constantly in some cases—someone will point out all the things in the world that just aren't fair.

True, it seems there's nothing worse than not receiving what you feel is rightfully yours and watching the least likely candidate get it instead. ❷ It's confusing, discouraging, and painful to watch "the rich get richer and the poor get poorer"—especially when you feel like the poorest among the poor. After a while you could begin to question your faith or doubt God's providence, His guidance in our lives and in the world. But a quick look at what the Bible has to say on the issue of fairness should put your anxieties to rest.

❶ What three-word cry is common to almost everyone?

Learning from the Bible ...

Psalm 37:3-9

Read the following Scripture in its entirety, pausing at the end of every verse so that students have to "wait" for you to continue.

Learning from the Bible

³ *Trust in the LORD and do what is good;*
dwell in the land and live securely.
⁴ *Take delight in the LORD,*
and He will give you your heart's desires.

⁵ *Commit your way to the LORD;*
trust in Him, and He will act,
⁶ *making your righteousness shine like the dawn,*
your justice like the noonday.

⁷ *Be silent before the LORD and wait expectantly for Him;*
do not be agitated by one who prospers in his way,
by the man who carries out evil plans.

⁸ *Refrain from anger and give up [your] rage;*
do not be agitated—it can only bring harm.
⁹ *For evildoers will be destroyed,*
but those who put their hope in the LORD
will inherit the land.

❷ What are five possible results of being overly concerned with what is and is not fair in the world?
1. Confusion
2. Discouragement
3. Personal pain
4. Questioning your faith
5. Doubting God's guidance in your life and the world

5

LARGE-GROUP TIME
CONTINUED:
This is the meat of the
teaching time. Remind
students to follow along
and take notes in their
Student Books.

As you share the
"So What?" information
with students, make
it your own. Use your
natural teaching style.
Emphasize underlined
information, which gives
key points with answers
to the *Student Book*
questions or fill-in-the-
blanks (shown in your
margins).

❸ Psalm 37 contrasts
the lives of the wicked
with those who seek to
live for God.

❹ What should you
do when you notice a
coworker chatting on
his cell in the stock-
room instead of work-
ing on the inventory?

❺ What does "delight
in the Lord" mean?

What are the condi-
tions of God's promise
in Psalm 37:4?

The Good, the Bad, and the Impatient

The psalmist uses 40 verses to address the same issues of fairness that concern people today. ❸ Psalm 37 contrasts the lives of the wicked with those who seek to live for God. It's a psalm that still has applications in our modern culture. The words God spoke to David continue to speak to us today.

The tendency we all face is to become bitter when we see good things happening to bad people. Someone in your class cheats and makes a high grade on the test after you prepared all week and pulled an all-nighter. The guy who only works when the boss is around gets the raise instead. The popular candidate who lies to get elected is voted class president. The list of injustices goes on and on.

It's tempting to watch and wait for cheaters to get caught, to get their due. ❹ But David says to stop watching impatiently for justice to be served. Instead, he says, "wait expectantly" on the Lord (v. 7).

Worth the Wait

Instead of being concerned with the good things happening to "the man who carries out evil plans" (v. 7)—cheating, slacking at work, obtaining a leadership position through deceit—we are to "do what is good" (v. 3) as Scripture teaches. If you put your trust in the Lord, He will replace your frustrations with thoughts of His love, mercy, and justice. With this perspective, you can get up every morning and go through your day without being concerned about whether Joe Lazy will get what's coming to him. God is aware of those who are after His heart. We can certainly trust Him.

When we let go of our anxieties, deciding instead to "delight in the Lord," God will give us the desires of our hearts (v. 4). You may think you know what delighting in God means, but let's be sure. ❺ Simply put, to take delight in the Lord means to make knowing and enjoying God your greatest joy and source of satisfaction. Sounds easy, doesn't it? The problem is that so many things look, sound, and feel good that we often grow distracted in our determination to find contentment in God. But nothing you can see, hear, or experience will ever really satisfy you. Only a relationship with Jesus can do that.

"So," you may ask, "What do I have to do to get my heart's desires?" Notice that verse 4 is conditional: ❻ "*If* you will delight in the Lord, then He will give you the desires of your heart" (emphasis added). If you find your greatest joy in knowing God, then your heart will come alive to all the things He has in store for you. He will create in you the desire for the things He wants for you—perhaps in the form of a new job or relationship that honors Him. When you focus on God, you are freed from selfish desires and worldly pursuits. You begin to think like Christ. You desi◼ the things that will bring glory to God. You pursue those things that have eternal benefits.

❼ What two things are you to do when you don't get what you want when you want it?
1. "Commit your way to the LORD."
2. "Be silent before the LORD and wait expectantly for Him."

❼ <u>But what are you supposed to do when you don't get what you want when you want it? (1) First, "Commit your way to the LORD" (v.5). (2) Then "Be silent befor◼ the LORD and wait expectantly for Him" (v.7).</u> Put God first. Don't complain to Hi◼ Try your best not to "be agitated by one who prospers" by doing evil (v.7). The wo◼ says that waiting is a waste of time, suggesting that you are better off to do thin◼ your way. But God says "wait expectantly." **❽** <u>Waiting is not a waste when you realize and trust that God is at work.</u> The worst thing you can do is to run ahead ◼ God's plans for you, trying to do life your own way. God wants you to depend on H◼ for everything. Waiting is a process God will use to develop your character. Remember, being angry and overly concerned with things you can't control will eventually catch up with you. The Bible tells you to let it go; give it up: "Give up [your] rage; do not be agitated—it can only bring harm" (v.8). "Evildoers will be destroyed, but those who put their hope in the LORD will inherit the land" (v.9).

❽ True or False: Waiting is a waste of time. (False)

Take care to consistently depend on God. Don't return to independence soon after◼ God meets your immediate needs. He doesn't want to be ignored in the times you◼ aren't in desperate need or want. Trust your life—your every day—to His capable hands.

SMALL-GROUP TIME:
Use this time to help
students begin to inte-
grate the truth they've
learned into their lives
while they connect with
other students in the
group, the leaders, and
with God.

Ask students to divide
back into small groups
and discuss the "Do
What?" questions.
Small-group facilitators
should lead the discus-
sions and set the model
for being open and
honest in responding to
questions.

Do What? *(15 MINUTES)*

Group Experience: How Do You Wait?

1. When you really want something, how many times a day do you pray to receive it?
   - ☐ I don't pray
   - ☐ Once
   - ☐ Twice
   - ☐ Three times
   - ☐ More than three times a day

2. When life seems great and you don't really need anything, how many times a day do you pray?
   - ☐ I don't pray every day
   - ☐ Once
   - ☐ Twice
   - ☐ Three times
   - ☐ More than three times a day

3. How do you usually react to unfair situations? Check all that apply.
   - ☐ I become angry and agitated.
   - ☐ I continue to do good things for God.
   - ☐ I trust in God's justice.
   - ☐ I complain to anyone who will listen.
   - ☐ I silently and expectantly wait before the Lord.

4. What is the most difficult thing about waiting on God? What is the greatest benefit?

LifePoint Review

Some of the greatest moments in your relationship with God are those when you stop thinking about you, choosing instead to let your mind and body rest in time spent alone with Him.

"Do" Points:

These "Do" Points will help you grab hold of this week's LifePoint. Be open and honest as you answer the questions within your small group.

1. <u>Prioritize your passions according to God's standards.</u> You will lose interest in the things you love most if you allow them to come before God. God alone brings meaning and fulfillment.
   How can you use the things you love most for God?

2. <u>Be faithful to do the little things while waiting for bigger things to come.</u> Great accomplishments for God result from faithfulness to the daily opportunities He provides.
   Why does it seem more important to tackle great things for God rather than investing in daily tasks that serve Him and others?

3. <u>Tell others about how God gives you your heart's desires.</u> One way you can encourage people and glorify God is by telling others of God's blessings on your life.
   When is the last time you told someone about God's blessings?

Prayer Connection:

Share prayer needs with the group, especially those related to your concern with unfairness in the world and delighting in God in spite of it. Your group facilitator will close your time in prayer.

Prayer Needs:

now What?

Encourage students to dig a little deeper by completing a "Now What?" assignment before the next time you meet. Remind students about the "Get Ready" short daily Bible readings and related questions at the beginning of Session 5.

Take it to the next level by completing one of these assignments this week:

Option #1:

List the ten things you love most. Post the list where you will see it every day. Tape it on your bathroom mirror or inside your locker at school. At the end of the week, determine how the items on your list fit into God's plan for your life. Mark off things that might keep you from being the person God wants you to be.

Option #2:

Specifically choose three acts of service that you can do to minister to others this week. Choose things that will keep you from receiving public recognition. If you can serve in secret, all the better. At the end of the week, evaluate how each of the things you did made you feel. Ask God to continue to use you to serve others as He prepares you for your future with Him.

Bible Reference Notes

Use these notes to deepen your understanding as you study the Bible on your own:

Psalm 37:3

trust in the Lord. This is a deep reliance on the God who promises to punish the ungodly and reward righteous.
the land. Many interpreters see Israel's promised land as a type of heaven (John 14:1–6).
enjoy safe pasture. God's people are often analogized as sheep, with Jesus as the Shepherd (John 10:27–29).

Psalm 37:4

Men and women who delight in God desire only what will please Him. The desires mentioned here are casual wishes but rather innermost desires.
heart. This refers to the center of the human spirit that produces emotions, thought, motivations, cou age, and action (see Prov. 4:23).

Psalm 37:5

Commit your way. This, literally, means "to roll it over on" the Lord. God's people can place the weigh of life upon the Lord (see Phil. 4:6–7).

Psalm 37:6

noonday sun. No shade of reproach or sin will remain.

Psalm 37:7

Be still ... wait patiently. To hush the spirit and to be silent before the Lord, knowing that God's timin is never wrong.

Psalm 37:8

do not fret. God's goodness is more evident in how He works through our troubles and defeats than i the successes of the wicked.

NOTES

NOTES

Session 5

THE WAY OF THE JOURNEY

Connections Prep

MAIN LIFEPOINT: Deciding to surrender your life to God's will means living by His values instead of the world's.

To reinforce the LifePoint, leaders and small group facilitators should understand the following more detailed CheckPoints and "Do" Points.

BIBLE STUDY CHECKPOINTS:
· Explain how Jesus gave His Father's will top priority
· Acknowledge the importance of surrendering to God's will
· Describe the value of seeking eternal treasures over earthly pleasures

LIFE CHANGE "DO" POINTS:
· List three things that threaten your loyalty to Christ
· Keep a journal of the difficult choices you make
· Pray for discernment in making the right choices

PREPARATION:
☐ Review the *Leader's Book* for the session and prepare your teaching.
☐ Determine how you will subdivide students into small discussion groups.
☐ Recruit mature students or adults as small-group facilitators. Be sure these facilitators plan to attend.
☐ Create a list of several unrelated persons or things such as the Queen of England, a porcupine, cotton candy, a freckle, and an octopus for the "Say What?" segment.

REQUIRED SUPPLIES:
☐ *Critical Decisions: Clarity in the Journey* leader book for each group facilitator
☐ *Critical Decisions: Clarity in the Journey* student book for each student
☐ Pen or pencil for each student
☐ List of several unrelated persons or things for "Say What?"

Get Ready

Spend a few moments getting to know God. Read one of these brief passages each day, and be sure to write down anything He reveals to you.

MONDAY

Read Philippians 2:5

Do you ever have a bad attitude? If so, what causes it? What adjustments can you make to have a more Christ-like attitude?

TUESDAY

Read Philippians 2:6-7

Have you ever acted super spiritual? How should knowing that Jesus temporarily gave up His place in heaven impact the way you live?

WEDNESDAY

Read Philippians 2:8

Are you an obedient person? How far would you go to obey God? What would you be willing to sacrifice for Him?

THURSDAY

Read Philippians 2:9

What kind of obedience and devotion does God require of you? Do you expect God reward you for your loyalty? If so, with what do you think He will reward you?

FRIDAY

Read Philippians 2:10

Do you think of Jesus more as a buddy or as the Lord? How do you think each helps your relationship with Him? How do you show Him respect and honor?

SATURDAY

Read Philippians 2:11

Is it natural for you to tell others about Christ? When you share your faith, do people take you seriously? In what ways—other than giving verbal testimony—do you acknowledge Christ as Lord of your life?

SUNDAY

Read Philippians 2:11

In addition to claiming Jesus as Lord of your life, do you also profess Him as Lord of heaven and earth? How does this truth influence the way you view the world?

5

 LifePoint

LARGE-GROUP OPENING:
t everyone's attention. Make announcements. pen your session with a prayer. Read the ePoint to the students.

Ask students to share bout last week's "Now What?" options. Ask m to explain anything they decided to drop m their lists of things y love most. Ask how they carried out their ndom acts of ministry. ere they able to keep low profiles? Did they have good attitudes?

Surrendering your life to God's will means living by His values instead of the world's.

SMALL-GROUP TIME:
Instruct students to
separate into smaller
groups of 4-8, prefer-
ably in a circle con-
figuration. Call on the
mature student or adult
leaders you recruited
to facilitate each small
group through this "Say
What?" segment.

 # Say What? *(15 MINUTES)*

Random Question of the Week:
Why are the sand dollars that wash up on the beach almost always broken?

Group Experience: Who Knows?

*(Permission is granted to copy only this page for use by facilitators as part of the
Life Connections® Youth Clarity in the Journey study.)*

Ask one student to step out of the room. From your list of unrelated persons or
things, assign an identity to the missing student. Say to the class, "OK, when
_____ comes back in, she is a(n) ... _____. Don't tell her what
she is."

Call the student back and tell her to select three students who will each ask one
question giving clues to her identity. For example, if she is an octopus, they might
ask: "How do you like living under water? Do you ever squirt your ink accidentally?
Do your arms tend to get stuck to things?" Instead of answering each question, the
student will try to guess her identity. If she hasn't correctly guessed after three
clues, reveal her identity. Repeat the exercise with a different student and a different object from your list.

1. How do clues help us find answers?

2. If you could have the answer to one particularly big question (such as whom you
   will marry), how might it change your life?

3. How would knowing God's will for you affect what you are doing and the plans
   you are making for the future?

So What? *(30 MINUTES)*

Teaching Outline

I. The Search for God's Will

    A. The search for God's will seems similar to a trek down the yellow-brick road

    B. Following God's will is easier than you might think

II. Learning from the Bible (Scripture)

III. What Is God's Will?

    A. God's will is what He wants you to be and do

    B. God's will is less complicated than some suggest

    C. God's will is not lost

IV. Jesus' Example of How to Live in the Will of God and Make Wise Decisions

    A. Jesus followed the will of God from the beginning

    B. Jesus daily surrendered His will to God's

    C. Jesus knew what was most important

5

The Search for God's Will

Who doesn't remember the story of Dorothy, a little girl who loses her way home and finds herself on an extraordinary journey? Though she and some rather unusual friends search all over fantastic Oz for a way to send her back to her aunt, Dorothy overlooks the possibility that she already holds the power to get back.

❶ For many of us, the search for God's will is similar to a journey down Dorothy's yellow brick road. You might not know where you are going, but you continue moving forward. You're not exactly sure what you are looking for, but you keep searching. You have an idea of what is at the end of the road, but you're not sure what to expect along the way. And worst of all, you don't know what you should do while moving closer to the end of the journey. ❷ Fortunately, following God's will is much easier than you might think—once you understand what God's will is.

Learning from the Bible ...

Philippians 2:5-11

Ask a student or adult skilled in dramatics to use interpretive movement or sign language to bring the words of the Scripture passage to life as you read it aloud.

LARGE-GROUP TIME CONTINUED:
This is the meat of the teaching time. Remind students to follow along and take notes in their *Student Books*.

As you share the "So What?" information with students, make it your own. Use your natural teaching style.

Emphasize underlined information, which answers to the Student Book questions or fill-in-the-blanks (shown in your margins).

❸ God's will is simply what God desires for you to do and become.

❹ God's will is not missing.

Learning from the Bible

⁵ *Make your own attitude that of Christ Jesus,*
⁶ *who, existing in the form of God, did not consider equality with God*
as something to be used for His own advantage.
⁷ *Instead He emptied Himself by assuming the form of a slave,*
taking on the likeness of men.
And when He had come as a man in His external form,
⁸ *He humbled Himself by becoming obedient to the point of death—even to death on a cross.*
⁹ *For this reason God also highly exalted Him and gave Him the name that is above every name,*
¹⁰ *so that at the name of Jesus every knee should bow—*
of those who are in heaven and on earth and under the earth—
¹¹ *and every tongue should confess that Jesus Christ is Lord,*
to the glory of God the Father.

What Is God's Will?

What does it mean to follow God's will? For that matter, what is God's will? An explanation of this important concept sometimes comes across like a research paper on how photosynthesis occurs. But ❸ God's will is simply what God desires for you to do and become.

One of the biggest mistakes Christians make is to search for God's will as if it w lost. But it's important to realize that ❹ God's will is not missing. We can stop searching for future events or revelations, instead committing ourselves to bein the men and women God wants us to be. Our job is to do the types of things we know He wants us to do.

When you are living your life for God, striving to live out what He desires for you, you are following God's will. In fact, you are right in the middle of it! Today's session will examine several principles from Jesus' life that will help you live in the will of God and make wise decisions.

Jesus' Example of How to Live in the Will of God and Make Wise Decisions

Before Jesus came to the world as a baby—even before the creation of the world—He existed with God in heaven. He was not in human form with all of its limitations, pain, and hardships; He was in the form of God. While Jesus could have remained where He was and never experienced life on earth, He "did not consider equality with God as something to be used for His own advantage" (v.6). It was Jesus' *choice* whether to remain with His Father in heaven or come to earth. He chose to follow the will of His Father. That's why He came.

Christ's "advantage" was to remain with God (since He is God) and avoid interaction with a sinful world. But He did what His Father wanted Him to do. He became who His father wanted Him to become: "He emptied Himself by assuming the form of a slave, taking on the likeness of men" (v.7). ❺ (1) From the beginning, Jesus decided to follow the will of God.

Jesus knew how His life on earth would play out. He knew that in order to become a man, He would have to let go of His status in heaven. He knew that His life would be full of pain and eventual torture. But in spite of it all, Jesus made a choice to lay aside His incomparable power and to take on humanity. In doing so, He showed us how to be servants who willingly serve the Father.

There are countless instances of Jesus being obedient to the will of God. ❺ (2) Jesus surrendered His will to God's on a daily basis. On one occasion, after feeding 5,000 families with what amounted to a fish and fries combo meal, the people (now full from the abundance of the miraculous food) were so impressed that they wanted to make Him their king. How great it would have been for Jesus to reclaim some of His glory—if even in an earthly sense. But He did not consider the offer. ❻ Instead, Jesus went away by Himself to a mountain (see John 6:1-15). He chose to resist the offer by removing Himself from the situation. He didn't come for earthly power. Jesus knew that following God's will for His life would accomplish far greater things. ❺ (3)He knew that following the will of God was the most important thing He could do.

On another occasion, one of Jesus' closest friends, Peter, verbally attacked Him about His impending death on the cross. Jesus responded to Peter with a rebuke. He even called him "Satan" because Peter was not thinking about God's plan but man's (Mark 8:33). ❼ Jesus knew that following God's will is far more important than pleasing people. That's why He willingly "humbled Himself by becoming obedient to the point of death—even to death on a cross" (vv. 7-8).

Sidebar (left margin):

List three ways Jesus showed us how to live in the will of God and make wise decisions.
Jesus followed the will of God from the beginning.
Jesus surrendered His will to God's on a daily basis.
Jesus knew what was most important.

❻ What was Jesus' response to those who wanted to make Him their king?
He accepted and was crowned King of the Jews
He preached a sermon on "The One True King"
He went to a mountain by Himself
He rebuked the people

❼ Jesus knew that it was far more important follow God's will than to ...
Please Himself
Please Peter
Please people
All of the above

Jesus willingly bypassed what He could gain on earth for your sake. All the way t the cross, Jesus knew that a treasure far more valuable than anything on earth awaited Him in heaven. "For this reason God also highly exalted Him and gave H the name that is above every name, so that at the name of Jesus every knee sho bow—of those who are in heaven and on earth and under the earth—and every tongue should confess that Jesus Christ is Lord, to the glory of God the Father" (9-11).

When you decide from the start to commit your life to God, you will have the joy a confidence of knowing that your Heavenly Father will guide and direct you in mal wise decisions.

SMALL-GROUP TIME:
Use this time to help
students focus on how
their lives can be dif-
ferent because of this
study as they connect
with the other students
in the group, the lead-
ers, and with God.

Ask students to divide
back into small groups
and discuss the "Do
What?" questions.
Small-group facilitators
should lead the discus-
sions and set the model
for being open and
honest in responding to
questions.

 # Do What? *(15 MINUTES)*

Group Experience: Like Christ

1. If you were in Jesus' shoes, which of the following would be most difficult for you?
   - ☐ Not using my divine power as a free pass to do things my way (v.6)
   - ☐ Humbling myself (v. 7,8)
   - ☐ Acting as a servant (v. 7)
   - ☐ Looking like any average human (v. 7)
   - ☐ Obeying God's will to the point of death (v. 8)

2. What is it about your character that makes it difficult to be like God wants you to be?

5

3. What is it about your conduct that makes it difficult for you to do what God wants you to do?

LifePoint Review

Surrendering your life to God's will means living by His values instead of the world's.

"Do" Points:

These "Do" Points will help you grab hold of this week's LifePoint. Be open and honest as you answer the questions within your small group.

1. <u>List three things that threaten your loyalty to Christ.</u> Many things can come between you and your relationship with Jesus.
   What persons, possessions, or obsessions are turning your loyalty away from Christ?

2. <u>This week, keep a journal of the difficult choices you make.</u> Some choices are simple but others are difficult to make on your own.
   What is the most difficult choice you're facing? How will it impact you and those you care about?

3. <u>Pray for discernment in making the right choices.</u> Sometimes you may make a good choice but not always the best one.
   How will you be able to determine whether or not you have made the best possible choice?

Prayer Connection:

This is the time to encourage, support, and pray for each other.

Share prayer needs with the group, especially those related to struggles in following God's will for you. Your group facilitator will close your time in prayer.

Prayer Needs:

Encourage students to dig a little deeper by completing a "Now What?" assignment before the next time you meet. Remind students about the "Get Ready" short daily Bible readings and related questions at the beginning of Session 6.

 now What?

Take it to the next level by completing one of these assignments this week:

Option #1:

Make a "First Will and Testament." List the personal resources you are willing to commit to God's use. Include time, talents, personal finances, and anything else that you can offer God. Use wording similar to, "Today (insert date) I give to God my (list resources) to be used by Him in anyway He decides." Sign it and have two mature Christians sign as witnesses to your commitment. Keep your "will" accessible so that you can measure your faithfulness to the commitments.

Option #2:

Copy Philippians 2:5-11 in your own handwriting every day this week. (No typing: that's cheating.) Each day, underline the quality of Christ that you find most difficult to imagine Him doing; circle the quality of Christ that you would most like to have; and complete the sentence, "My attitude is …".

5

Bible Reference Notes

Use these notes to deepen your understanding as you study the Bible on your own:

Philippians 2:6-11

There is little agreement between scholars as to how this hymn breaks into verses or how it is to be phrased. However, one thing is clear. The hymn has two equal parts. Part one (vv. 6–8) focuses on the self-humiliation of Jesus. Part two (vv. 9–11) focuses on God's exaltation of Jesus. In part one, Jesus the subject of the two main verbs, while in part two God is the subject of the two main verbs.

Philippians 2:6

being. This is not the normal Greek word for "being." This word carries the idea of preexistence. By using it, Paul is saying Jesus always existed in the form of God.
very nature. The Greek word is *morphe* (used twice by Paul in this hymn). He says Jesus was "in very nature God," and He then took upon Himself "the very nature of a servant." This is a key word in understanding the nature of Christ.
to be grasped. This is a rare word, used only at this point in the New Testament. It refers to the fact that Jesus did not have to "snatch" equality with God. Equality was not something He needed to acquire. It was His already, and He could give it away. Giving, not grasping, is what Jesus did.

Philippians 2:7

made himself nothing. Literally, "to empty," or "to pour out until the container is empty."
taking the very nature of a servant. Jesus gave up Godhood and took on slavehood. From being the ultimate master, He became the lowest servant. He left ruling for serving.
being made. In contrast to the verb in verse 6 (that stresses Christ's eternal nature), this verb points the fact that at a particular time He was born in the likeness of a human being.
human likeness. Jesus did not just seem to be human. He assumed the identity and flesh of a human being and was similar in all ways to other human beings.

Philippians 2:8

in appearance as a man. The word translated "in appearance" is *schema* and denotes that which is outward and changeable (distinct from *morphe*, which denotes that which is essential and eternal).
he humbled himself. This is the central point of one who lived a life of self-sacrifice, self-renunciation and self-surrender.
obedient to death. The extent of this humbling is defined by this clause. Jesus humbled Himself to the furthest point one can go. He submitted to death itself for the sake of both God and humanity. There was not a more dramatic way to demonstrate humility.
death on a cross. This was no ordinary death. Crucifixion was a harsh, demeaning, and utterly painful way to die. According to the Old Testament, those who died by hanging on a tree were considered to have been cursed by God.

Philippians 2:9

name. In the ancient world, a name was more than just a way of distinguishing one individual from another. It revealed the inner nature or character of a person. The name given the resurrected Jesus the supreme name—the name above all names—because this is Jesus' identity in His innermost be

Philippians 2:10

bow. Everyone will one day pay homage to Jesus. This worship will come from all of creation—all ang (in heaven), all people (on earth), and all demons (under the earth).

Philippians 2:11

Jesus Christ is Lord. The climax of this hymn. This is the earliest and most basic confession of faith the part of the church (see Acts 2:36; Rom. 10:9; 1 Cor. 12:3).
Lord. This is the name that was given to Jesus; the name that reflects who He really is (see v. 9). The the name of God. Jesus is the supreme Sovereign of the universe.

Session

6

THE WRONG WAY

Connections Prep

MAIN LIFEPOINT:
In order to receive His grace and forgiveness when we sin, we must respond to God through confession and repentance.

To reinforce the LifePoint, leaders and small group facilitators should understand the following more detailed CheckPoints and "Do" Points.

BIBLE STUDY CHECKPOINTS:
· Understand that our sins have consequences
· Explain how God responds to us when we sin
· Demonstrate how we should respond to God when we sin

LIFE CHANGE "DO" POINTS:
· Confess to God the sin in your life
· Accept God's forgiveness for our mistakes
· Ask a trusted, mature Christian to pray with you about your most difficult struggles

PREPARATION:
☐ Review the *Leader's Book* for the session and prepare your teaching.
☐ Determine how you will subdivide students into small discussion groups.
☐ Recruit mature students or adults as small-group facilitators. Be sure these facilitators plan to attend.
☐ Wear a shirt with a visible spot on it that will immediately come out with a laundry stain remover.
☐ Provide a laundry stain remover stick or spray.
☐ Find several big, thick books.

REQUIRED SUPPLIES:
☐ *Critical Decisions: Clarity in the Journey* leader book for each group facilitator
☐ *Critical Decisions: Clarity in the Journey* student book for each student
☐ Pen or pencil for each student
☐ Shirt with a removable spot
☐ Laundry stain remover stick or spray
☐ Three or four large, thick books
☐ Stopwatch

This "Get Ready" section is primarily for the students, but leaders & facilitators will benefit from these devotionals as well.

 Get Ready

Spend a few moments getting to know God. Read one of these brief passages each day, and be sure to write down anything He reveals to you.

MONDAY

Read Hebrews 12:1

What keeps you from being effective in your witness for Christ? What sins hurt your relationship with God? Have you confessed them? If so, why do you think they keep tripping you up?

TUESDAY

Read Hebrews 12:2

What motivates the things you do, the things you say, and the relationships you pursue? How obvious is your devotion to Christ to others?

WEDNESDAY

Read Hebrews 12:3

Do you ever get tired of living the way God expects you to? Do you think Jesus ever grew weary of fulfilling His purpose on earth? How does Jesus' example encourage you to follow God in spite of circumstances?

THURSDAY

Read Hebrews 12:4

What has resisting temptation cost you? What was the most difficult spiritual struggle you ever experienced? What was the outcome of that situation?

FRIDAY

Read Hebrews 12:5-8

Do you ever feel like a child of God? What have you done that has resulted in God's discipline? What form has His discipline taken?

SATURDAY

Read Hebrews 12:9-10

How do your parents discipline you? When is the last time they did? How do you respond to discipline?

SUNDAY

Read Hebrews 12:11

Can you remember a time when you actually felt blessed when disciplined? How has discipline benefited you?

LARGE-GROUP OPENING:
t everyone's attention.
Make announcements.
pen your session with
a prayer. Read the
ePoint to the students.

Ask students to share
bout last week's "Now
What?" options. Ask
em to share how com-
mitted they have been
 giving God the things
romised in their "First
Will and Testament."
sk them to share their
eactions to writing out
the text of Philippians
2:5-11 multiple times.
What did they learn
about God's will by
meditating on the text
throughout the week?

 LifePoint

G

In order to receive His grace and forgiveness when we sin, we must respond to God through confession and repentance.

SMALL-GROUP TIME:
Instruct students to separate into smaller groups of 4-8, preferably in a circle configuration. Call on the mature student or adult leaders you recruited to facilitate each small group through the "Say What?" segment.

 # Say What? *(15 MINUTES)*

Random Question of the Week:
Why do fans *sit* in the *stands* at a football game?

Group Experience: Coming Clean
(Permission is granted to copy only this page for use by facilitators as part of the Life Connections® Youth Clarity in the Journey study.)

Wear the shirt with the visible stain. Begin to talk about sin, the bad things that separate us from God. Share that sin is like a stain on a white garment. If someone hasn't already commented on it, point out the stain on your shirt. Then, take the stain remover and remove the spot. Talk about how Christ alone can remove the sin from our lives so that we can enjoy our relationships with God.

1. What sins are most visible? Which are easiest to keep hidden?

2. When are you most aware of the sin in your life?

3. What decisions result from your awareness of sin?

So What? *(30 MINUTES)*

Teaching Outline

I. Rules, Rules, Rules
A. Your parents' job is to help you learn to follow the rules
B. Rules exist everywhere
C. There will always be rules and rule-givers

II. Learning from the Bible (Scripture)

III. What the Bible Says about Sin
A. Sin is the ungodly things you think, say, and do
B. Sin is missing the bull's eye
C. Sin has consequences

IV. God's Response to Sin
A. God wants you to avoid sin
B. God will discipline you
C. God will always love you

V. Our Response to God
A. Turn from sin
B. Turn to God

EACHING FOR THE
LARGE GROUP:
hare the "So What?"
ching with your stu-
ents. You may modify
to meet your needs.

Be sure to highlight
the underlined infor-
mation, which gives
swers to the *Student*
k questions and fill-
the-blanks (shown in
your margins).

❶ What is one thing
your parents do that
reflects God's role in
your life?

Rules, Rules, Rules
❶ <u>Until you're old enough to understand how to follow rules, one of your parents'</u> <u>many jobs is to protect you.</u> (And even after you understand the rules, they are still watching out for you.) They make sure the rungs on your crib are just the right size so you can't squeeze through them and end up on the floor. They put gates at both the bottom and top of stairs so you won't bump down them on your padded baby bottom. They pull you away from the stove—usually with a quick slap on your padded bottom—and they pull you away from the street—usually with a tight embrace. As you get older, parents begin to tell you not to do things—fully expect-ing you to obey them.

Then it's time to spread your wings. There are rules about riding your bike, riding in cars with friends, and then about driving your own car. In addition to those, yo gain other rule-givers like teachers, coaches, and highway patrolmen. There are rules at school, team rules, and rules about how fast you can drive. If you drive fast you'll get a ticket. If you don't come to practice, you'll get cut from the team If you cheat on a test, you'll get detention. And, yes, if you fall down the stairs— you'll still get hurt.

One day, when you are an adult, there will be rules on your job, in your neighborhood, and rules to govern golf, swimming, and tennis. ❷ There are three things that you can count on: rules, rule-givers, and consequences for breaking the rule Today we'll look at Hebrews 12:1-11 to see our Heavenly Father's actions and atti tudes toward us—His children—when we the critical decision to break the rules

Learning from the Bible

¹ Therefore since we also have such a large cloud of witnesses surrounding us, let us lay aside every weight and the sin that so easily ensnares us, and run with endurance the ra that lies before us, ² keeping our eyes on Jesus, the source and perfecter of our faith, w for the joy that lay before Him endured a cross and despised the shame, and has sat dow at the right hand of God's throne.

³ For consider Him who endured such hostility from sinners against Himself, so that you won't grow weary and lose heart. ⁴ In struggling against sin, you have not yet resisted to the point of shedding your blood. ⁵ And you have forgotten the exhortation that addresse you as sons:

> *My son, do not take the Lord's discipline lightly,*
> *or faint when you are reproved by Him;*
> *⁶ for the Lord disciplines the one He loves,*
> *and punishes every son whom He receives.*

⁷ Endure it as discipline: God is dealing with you as sons. For what son is there whom a father does not discipline? ⁸ But if you are without discipline—which all receive—then y are illegitimate children and not sons. ⁹ Furthermore, we had natural fathers discipline u and we respected them. Shouldn't we submit even more to the Father of spirits and live? ¹⁰ For they disciplined us for a short time based on what seemed good to them, but He d it for our benefit, so that we can share His holiness. ¹¹ No discipline seems enjoyable at time, but painful. Later on, however, it yields the fruit of peace and righteousness to thos who have been trained by it.

❷ **List three things related to following directions that you can count on:**
1. rules
2. rule-givers
3. consequences for breaking the rules

Learning from the Bible ...

Hebrews 12:1-11

Ask three students to read the Scripture aloud in unison. Enlist a fourth student to comment on their reading. After the students read the first two verses, the fourth should say, "Read verses three through six *slowly*." After they've done so, he will tell the students to read verses seven through eleven in a British accent. After the students have finished reading, comment that there are obviously even rules for reading Scripture.

ARGE-GROUP TIME
CONTINUED:
his is the meat of the
aching time. Remind
dents to follow along
d take notes in their
Student Books.

As you share the
o What?" information
with students, make
t your own. Use your
atural teaching style.
ou may modify it with
your own perspec-
tives and teaching
eeds. Emphasize the
derlined information,
ich gives key points,
iswers to the *Student*
k questions or fill-in-
blanks in the (shown
in your margins).

❸ Check the
statements that help
define sin.

❹ True or False?
mans 6:23 says that
the penalty of sin is
loneliness. (False)

❺ List four things out-
e the promise of eter-
l life, that sin affects.
elationships
reams
eputation
eace

For what two reasons
does God want you to
completely avoid sin?

What the Bible Says about Sin

No one likes to get into trouble; and if you follow the rules of your parents, teachers, and coaches, you'll be well on your way to staying out of it. But it's not always that easy. Sometimes you make poor choices that hurt others and yourself. Even talking about someone behind her back can hurt reputations and your character. One of the worst choices you can make in the journey is deliberately doing something you know is wrong. ❸ When you think, say, or do something that is not in God's plan for you, it is sin. Sin means missing the mark of God's righteousness and holiness.

Imagine playing darts. The goal is to hit the bull's eye. Every time you miss that mark, it's like committing a sin. Sin is missing the best plan—the bull's eye—that God has for you. It keeps us from living in holiness and righteousness as God desires.

❹ But sin is far more serious than our dart game illustration might suggest. Paul says, "The wages of sin is death, but the gift of God is eternal life in Christ Jesus our Lord" (Rom. 6:23). God's original plan was for humanity to live forever with Him in Eden. But once Adam and Eve sinned, humankind lost that privilege.

Before you place your faith in Christ, your spirit is dead because of sin. You are destined not to an eternity in heaven with Christ, but to an eternity of separation from Him in Hell. You are in a broken relationship with God. ❺ This is why sin can also lead to the death of those things you most cherish: relationships, dreams, reputation, and peace. Sin separates you from God, blocking your way to true joy and satisfaction.

God's Response to Sin

Have you ever done something and hoped no one would discover it? Have you ever breathed a sigh of relief because you only thought evil—thankful that you didn't act on it? God knows your thoughts; He is aware of your actions. ❻ God wants you to completely avoid sin, not only because of the way it can wreck your life, but also because of the way it prevents others from seeing Jesus in you. Like a parent intent on keeping his baby from harm, God watches you like a loving Father.

So what does God do when those who claim to follow Him sin? The Bible says that God loves you and has provided a way for you to experience forgiveness through the faith you have placed in His Son. It instructs that you keep your eyes on Jesus, "the source and perfecter of our faith, who for the joy that lay before Him endured a cross and despised the shame, and has sat down at the right hand of God's throne" (v. 2). Don't get discouraged. Ask for forgiveness again and again.

❼ How does God show His love to you?

❽ True or False: God turns all of your experiences into growth opportunities. (True)

Remember all that Jesus went through for you and be encouraged to follow His example. Furthermore, expect that ❼ <u>God will show you His love through discipli as each of us is faced with critical decisions throughout our days and weeks.</u> In verses 7-11 the writer of Hebrews compares God's discipline to the way parents cipline children: God's discipline, like that of our parents, might not be pleasant experience at the time. Later on, however, it yields the fruit of peace and righteou ness to those who have been trained by it.

As your Eternal Parent, your Heavenly Father, ❽ <u>God turns all of your experiences i growth opportunities.</u> Romans 8:28 reminds you that God uses *all* things for His go

Your Response to God

❾ According to Hebrews 12:1, what are we supposed to do with sin?

☐ Trust God to make it go away.

☐ Ignore it

☐ Lay it aside

☐ Embrace it

❿ What are the two parts of true repentance?

Sometimes you are convicted in your heart to turn from things you think, say, or that are not what God desires of you; but doing so requires discipline. ❾ <u>Hebrew 12:1 says to "lay aside every weight and the sin that so easily ensnares us." Tha means taking whatever habit or temptation you are likely to give in to, and laying aside.</u> It means throwing it as far away as you can, avoiding it.

God knows that sin will hinder your faith and effectiveness for Him. That's why yo are to keep your "eyes on Jesus, the source and perfecter of our faith, who for the joy that lay before Him endured a cross and despised the shame, and has sat do at the right hand of God's throne" (vv. 1-2) ❿ <u>These verses contain the two part true repentance. First, it requires that you stop your current sinful behavior, turni your back on it. You have to see your sin the way God sees your sin—something be avoided. Second, you must turn to God and trust that He loves you so much th He will forgive you.</u>

SMALL-GROUP TIME:
Use this time to help
students begin to inte-
grate the truth they've
learned into their lives
while they connect with
other students in the
group, the leaders, and
with God.

Ask students to divide
back into small groups
and discuss the "Do
What?" questions.
Small-group facilitators
should lead the discus-
sions and set the model
for being open and
honest in responding to
questions.

D.o What? *(15 MINUTES)*

Group Experience: Weighed Down

Ask a student to sit in a chair and raise his legs straight out in front of him. Place one of the big books your brought on his legs, and see how long he can keep his legs up. When his legs fall, add another book. Then repeat with a third. Time how long he can hold his legs up under each added weight. The times will get shorter and shorter as your volunteer runs out of strength.

1. How did the additional weight affect the strength of his legs?

2. How might the books represent sin?

3. How did his endurance represent resisting temptation?

4. What sins are keeping you giving your best for God?

LifePoint Review

In order to receive His grace and forgiveness when we sin, we must respond to God through confession and repentance.

"Do" Points:

These "Do" Points will help you grab hold of this week's LifePoint. Be open and honest as you answer the questions within your small group.

1. <u>Confess to God the sins in your life.</u> Don't try to hide anything from Him. God knows your thoughts.
   What specific sins do you need to confess? Do any of them keep showing back up in your life, even though you've repeatedly given them over to God?

2. <u>Accept God's forgiveness for sins committed this week.</u> If you confess your sins—any and all sins—God will forgive you.
   Do you have a difficult time accepting God's forgiveness? If so, is it because you feel unworthy or because you doubt God's promises?

3. <u>Ask a trusted, mature Christian to pray with you about the sin with which you most struggle.</u> God places people in your life to help you deal with the things that are bigger than you are. Sin is bigger than all of us, but we can find strength and accountability in each other.
   Whom will you contact to be your prayer partner?

Prayer Connection:

This is the time to encourage, support, and pray for each other as you confront and confess the sin in your life. Remember, true repentance brings God's forgiveness.

Share prayer needs with the group, especially those related to personal sin and repentance. Your group facilitator will close your time in prayer.

Prayer Needs:

now What?

Encourage students to dig a little deeper by completing a "Now What?" assignment before the next time you meet. Remind students about the "Get Ready" short daily Bible readings and related questions at the beginning of Session 7.

Take it to the next level by completing the "Now What?" assignment this week:

Neatly fold a piece of paper so it's easy to carry with you. Place it in a book at school, a Bible, or keep it neatly folded in your pocket or purse. During the week, tear the paper each time you become aware of a sin in your life. Then fold it and return it to your pocket, purse, or book. At the end of the week, note the number of tears in the paper. Ask yourself, *If the paper represents my relationship with God and the tears represent sin in my life, what must my relationship with God look like after seven days?* (Remember God's promise to forgive you of your sin.)

Bible Reference notes

Use these notes to deepen your understanding as you study the Bible on your own:

G

Hebrews 12:1
witnesses. This is the same word as the one for "martyrs." It is probably a deliberate play on words in which both meanings are intended. The heroes of faith are pictured as a cheering section of former runners, urging contemporary runners to keep on as they did.
throw off everything. In Greek games at the time, runners ran naked so that no clothes would hinder their movement.
the sin that so easily entangles. Just as a flowing robe makes it impossible to run, so sin prevents one from pursuing Christ.

Hebrews 12:2
fix our eyes on Jesus. In races of the time, the prize for the race was placed at the end to motivate the runners. Jesus is here described as the prize upon which we are to focus.
joy set before him. Jesus knew the joy His mission of reconciliation would bring, and so pursued it whatever the cost. The readers are to follow that model.
scorning its shame. Crucifixion was considered so degrading that no Roman citizen could be crucified regardless of the crime committed.

Hebrews 12:3
Consider him. Instead of seeing opposition as an excuse to abandon faith, they should look to Jesus as a model of how to live faithfully through it.
weary and lose heart. These words were used in athletic circles to describe the collapse of a runner.

Hebrews 12:4
shedding your blood. The persecution they have experienced so far has not yet included the ultimate sacrifice made by Jesus.

Hebrews 12:7-11
A quote from Proverbs 3:11–12 (from the Septuagint), used to substantiate the author's point. At this time, corporal punishment of children was seen as a sign of a father's concern that his children learn right from wrong. Although children whose parents do not train or restrict them in any way seem to have more freedom, it is the children whose parents love them enough to administer discipline that grow into mature, responsible adults. In the same way, hardship is seen as a sign of God's care, since such discipline leads to growth in righteousness and peace.

NOTES

Session

7

NAVIGATING THE JOURNEY

Connections Prep

MAIN LIFEPOINT: Knowing God and submitting to His authority in all decisions results in ultimate freedom.

To reinforce the LifePoint, leaders and small-group facilitators should understand the following more detailed CheckPoints and "Do" Points.

BIBLE STUDY CHECKPOINTS:
· Understand the consequences of making decisions apart from God's authority
· Acknowledge that ultimate freedom results from placing our lives under God's authority

LIFE CHANGE "DO" POINTS:
· List the positives and negatives of being under authority
· List from Scripture the most difficult of God's commands to follow. Ask Him to give you the willingness to obey them
· Spend time each day learning more about God's rich complexity and depth.

PREPARATION:
☐ Review the *Leader's Book* for this session and prepare your teaching.
☐ Determine how you will subdivide students into small discussion groups.
☐ Recruit mature students or adults as small-group facilitators. Be sure these facilitators plan to attend.

REQUIRED SUPPLIES:
☐ *Critical Decisions: Clarity in the Journey* leader book for each group facilitator
☐ *Critical Decisions: Clarity in the Journey* student book for each student
☐ Pen or pencil for each student

This "Get Ready" section is primarily for the students, but leaders & facilitators will benefit from these devotionals as well.

Get Ready

Spend a few moments getting to know God. Read one of these brief passages each day, and be sure to write down anything He reveals to you.

MONDAY

Read Genesis 2:15
What responsibilities do your parents give you? How do your present responsibilit differ from those you had as a small child?

TUESDAY

Read Genesis 2:16-17
How much freedom do your parents allow you? Is it enough? How do you define "freedom"? Do you think you should have more?

WEDNESDAY

Read Genesis 3:1
Do personal thoughts or other people ever cause you to doubt God's Word?

THURSDAY

Read Genesis 3:2-3
How do you combat temptation? Do you find it easy to recall the commands of Go Why might someone choose not to trust in His promises?

FRIDAY

Read Genesis 3:4
What lie has the world fed you? What temptation most commonly captures your attention? Do you trust God's power to permanently remove that temptation from your life?

SATURDAY

Read Genesis 3:5

Are there times when you want to be like God? In what ways would it be impossible for you to be like Him? What problems might this pose?

SUNDAY

Read Genesis 3:6

How far would you go to get what you want? How many of your temptations are related to things you see? Do you think you would be tempted less if you didn't have the use of your eyes?

**LARGE-GROUP
OPENING:**
everyone's attention.
ake announcements.
en your session with
a prayer. Read the
Point to the students.

Ask students to share
out last week's "Now
at?" option. Ask them
to describe how their
papers looked at the
of seven days. Were
re many tears? Were
he papers shredded?

 LifePoint

Knowing God and submitting to His authority in all things results in ultimate freedom.

87

Say What? *(15 MINUTES)*

Random Question of the Week:
What is a soufflé, and how do you make one?

Group Experience: Do You Trust Me?

(Permission is granted to copy only this page for use by facilitators as part of th
Life Connections® Youth Clarity in the Journey study.)

Ask for a volunteer to stand in the center of the group. Ask the student if he trus
you. Then ask if he *really* trusts you. Tell the student to close his eyes. Stand two
feet behind the student and tell him to extend his arms so that they are parallel
with the floor. Tell him to fall backwards. Catch the student securely by slipping
your arms under his outstretched arms.

1. How easy is it to trust someone?

2. What would a person have to do to earn your complete trust?

3. Does knowing a person increase or decrease your trust in him?

4. How might submitting to God result in freedom and trust?

So What? *(30 MINUTES)*

Teaching Outline

I. Who's in Charge?

A. To be successful, you must accept the role and authority of the person in charge

B. You have multiple authority figures in your life

C. Be careful not to become your own authority figure

II. Learning from the Bible (Scripture)

III. Put God in Charge

A. No one likes to be told what to do

B. Some people try to remove themselves from God's authority

C. Christian maturity is seen in your willingness to place yourself under God's authority

IV. God Rules

A. God intended the world to be a free place to live

B. Sin took that freedom away

C. Where there is danger, there are rules

D. God has put up "fences" to protect us

7

Who's in Charge?

The most successful players—be they on the field, the stage, or in the orchestra pit—are those who accept the role and authority of the person in charge. ❶ It is difficult to give your best effort if you don't trust the person over you, following his or her plans for your team, troupe, or band. But whether or not you choose to recognize authority, there will always be people to whom you must answer. First parents, then teachers, then bosses. And instead of gaining fewer authority figures in your life as you grow older, oddly enough, you'll seem to accumulate more while also gaining more and more independence. ❷ With so many "bosses" in your life, it may seem easier to ignore them and be your own authority instead. But beware of trying to assert yourself in the presence of someone far more qualified than you:

89

"The lion was proud of his mastery of the animal kingdom. One day he decided to make sure all the other animals knew he was the king of the jungle. He was s confident that he bypassed the smaller animals and went straight to the bear. 'is king of the jungle?' the lion asked. The bear replied, 'Why, you are, of course.' The lion gave a mighty roar of approval.

"Next he asked the tiger, 'Who is the king of the jungle?' The tiger quickly respond 'Everyone knows that you are, O mighty lion.'

"Next on the list was the elephant. The lion faced the elephant and addressed h question: 'Who is the king of the jungle?' The elephant immediately grabbed the lion with his trunk, whirled him around in the air five or six times, and slammed him into a tree. Then he pounded him on the ground several times, dunked him under water in a nearby lake, and finally threw him onto the shore.

"The lion—beaten, bruised and battered—struggled to his feet. He looked at th elephant through sad and bloody eyes and said, 'Look, just because you don't kn the answer is no reason for you to get mean about it!'" [1]

Today's session will show the value of placing your life under God's authority. The you will find ultimate freedom.

Learning from the Bible

Learning from the Bible ...

Genesis 2:15-17; 3:1-6

Ask four volunteers to come to the front and read the parts of (1) the narrator, (2) God, (3) the serpent, and the (4) woman.

[NARRATOR] [15] *The Lord God took the man and placed him in the garden of Eden to wo and watch over it.* [16] *And the Lord God commanded the man,*

[GOD] *"You are free to eat from any tree of the garden,* [17] *but you must not eat from the tree of the knowledge of good and evil, for on the day you eat from it, you will certainly die."*

[NARRATOR] [1] *Now the serpent was the most cunning of all the wild animals that the L God had made. He said to the woman,*

[SERPENT] *"Did God really say, 'You can't eat from any tree in the garden'?"*

[NARRATOR] [2] *The woman said to the serpent,*

[1] James S. Hewitt, editor, *Illustrations Unlimited* (Wheaton, IL: Tyndale House Publishers, 1988), 312.

ARGE-GROUP TIME CONTINUED:

his is the meat of the eaching time. Remind dents to follow along nd take notes in their *Student Books.*

As you share the o What?" information with students, make it your own. Use your atural teaching style.

mphasize <u>underlined</u> rmation, which gives ey points, answers to the *Student Book* uestions or fill-in-the- anks in the (shown in your margins).

❸ God wants you to ek <u>Him</u> first, placing His will <u>first</u> in your life.

❹ <u>Maximum</u> freedom mes from <u>submitting</u> to God's rule over your life.

❺ Which of the llowing is most valu- able to you?

▶My freedom

▶My future

▶My education

▶My friends

❻ What is the differ- nce between parental authority and God's authority?

[WOMAN] "We may eat the fruit from the trees in the garden. ³ But about the fruit of the tree in the middle of the garden, God said, 'You must not eat it or touch it, or you will die.'"

[SERPENT] ⁴ "No! You will not die,"

[NARRATOR] the serpent said to the woman.

[SERPENT] ⁵ "In fact, God knows that when you eat it your eyes will be opened and you will be like God, knowing good and evil."

[NARRATOR] ⁶ Then the woman saw that the tree was good for food and delightful to look at, and that it was desirable for obtaining wisdom. So she took some of its fruit and ate [it]; she also gave [some] to her husband, [who was] with her, and he ate [it].

Put God in Charge

❸ <u>God wants you to seek Him first, placing His will first in your life.</u> When you do, living under His authority becomes a delight! You can tell that the psalmist had personally experienced the wonder of placing his will under the Lord's. Listen to his longing for more of God's influence in Psalm 119:10,12: "I have sought You with all my heart; don't let me wonder from Your commands ... LORD, may You be praised; teach me Your statutes." Once you get a taste of God's love, His commands become a joy because you know and trust in the One commanding you. ❹ <u>In fact, you'll learn that maximum freedom comes from submitting to God's rule over your life.</u>

Most people, if given the choice, might have a difficult time choosing between total independence and total freedom. ❺ <u>For many individuals, little is more valuable than independence.</u> Consider your own situation. Doesn't it seem that if you only had more freedom to make your own decisions, everything else would be fine?

Sometimes the opinions of trusted authority figures are the last thing you want to hear. That's unfortunate because God has placed these people in our lives and they have much to offer in the way of advice and counsel. As hard as it may be to believe, they too were once teens. They survived the years that you now face.

As you mature into adulthood—and eventually into parenthood—you naturally and rightfully step out from under parental authority. The Christian life, however, is somewhat different where authority is concerned. ❻ <u>You may get out from under the authority of your parents, but you will never be out from under the authority of God.</u> Many Christians, young and old, think they can make wise decisions without God's counsel. These unfortunately independent souls do not wish to acknowledge

7

❼ For the Christ-fol-
lower, true maturity is
seen in your <u>willingness</u>
to place your life under
God's <u>authority</u>, as you
make <u>choices</u> that coincide with His will and
direction for your life.

❽ How is living apart
from God's authority
like taking a train off its
tracks?

❾ True or False: Adam
and Eve could only stay
in the garden if they
followed a long list of
rules. (False)

❿ When did Adam and
Eve lose their freedom?

⓫ Why does God give
us rules?

God as the final authority on any matter. **❼** <u>But for the Christ-follower, true mat
rity is seen in your willingness to place your life under God's authority as you ma
choices that coincide with His will and direction for your life.</u>

Many people have a problem with being told what to do. They don't want to shar
control over their lives with anyone—especially not a God they choose to ignore.
The world tempts you with many alternate paths to freedom. Proverbs 14:12 warr
"There is a way that seems right to a man, but its end is the ways to death." The
world may tempt you to remove yourself from under *all* authority—earthly and
heavenly. "Only then," some might insist, "will you find freedom." **❽** <u>But the tru
is that such an approach is like removing a train from its tracks but still expecti
it to arrive at its destination. In reality, a person who does life without God's help
as destined for disaster as a derailed train.</u> True freedom comes when we choose
remain under God's authority. True freedom is moving easy in the harness.

God Rules

❾ <u>For a brief time, Adam and Eve were living in a world with but one rule:</u>, "You
are free to eat from any tree of the garden, but you must not eat from the tree of
the knowledge of good and evil, for on the day you eat from it, you will certainly c
(vv. 16-17). By His original plan, it is obvious that God has always been an advo
cate of freedom. That's why He allowed Adam and Eve so much of it. As long as t
enjoyed the garden under His authority, they had to follow just one rule.

Genesis 3 reads like a script of a play. **❿** <u>The serpent led Eve to believe that Goo
was hiding something good from her. The serpent even told Eve how she could ge
it: disobey. Only when Eve and Adam removed themselves from God's protective
umbrella of authority, choosing to heed the serpent's lies, did they land into a he
of trouble and the loss of freedom.</u> They didn't gain good things; they lost them.
Instead of one rule, they brought down rules, rules, and more rules on their own
heads. In fact, freedom was replaced with rules. God had to add more rules beca
life became more dangerous. **⓫** <u>God has put up fences to protect you, rather tha
to restrict your freedom. His rules exist for your protection.</u>

God didn't turn the world into a world of rules. Humanity's freedom to choose did
God does not take away freedom. Living apart from His authority makes you lose

Do What? *(15 MINUTES)*

MALL-GROUP TIME:
Use this time to help
tudents begin to inte-
grate the truth they've
arned into their lives
ile they connect with
other students in the
oup, the leaders, and
with God.

Ask students to divide
ack into small groups
and discuss the "Do
What?" questions.
nall-group facilitators
ould lead the discus-
ns and set the model
for being open and
nest in responding to
questions.

Group Experience: The Choice is Yours

1. Why do you think God made sure that Adam and Even knew the consequences of disobeying Him?

    ☐ He wanted to protect them.

    ☐ He wanted to show them how fair He is.

    ☐ He wanted to prepare them for temptation.

    ☐ He wanted them to appreciate their freedom.

    ☐ He wanted them to understand sin.

    ☐ Other: _____

2. What should you immediately do when tempted?

    ☐ Ask your friends for advice.

    ☐ Talk to your parents about it.

    ☐ Ask God to give you the strength to resist.

    ☐ Ask God for wisdom to know how to handle it.

    ☐ Quote an appropriate Bible verse.

    ☐ Ignore it.

    ☐ Other: _____

3. To what authority figures do you have the most difficult time submitting? Why?

4. How willingly do you submit to God's authority? How might someone see that you are submissive to God's will?

Small-group facilitators should reinforce the LifePoint for this session. Make sure that students' questions are invited and addressed honestly.

LifePoint Review

Knowing God and submitting to His authority in all things results in ultimate freed

"Do" Points:

These "Do" Points will help you grab hold of this week's LifePoint. Be open and honest as you answer the questions within your small group.

1. <u>List the positives and negatives of being under someone else's authority.</u> You always be subject to someone. If not your parents, a teacher, coach, or boss.
   What would be the worst thing that could happen to you if you totally subm ted to God's authority?

2. <u>List from Scripture the most difficult of God's commands to follow. Ask Him to give you the willingness to obey them.</u> God's Word is full of promises of love a forgiveness. It also contains some tough commands.
   Which of God's commands is most difficult for you to obey? Why?

3. <u>Daily spend time getting to better know God.</u> You spend time with the people y care about and enjoy being with.
   How much time do you spend with God each day? What might that suggest about your relationship with Him? What does it say about your commitment

Be sure to end your session by asking students to share prayer needs with one another, especially as they relate to issues brought up by today's session.

Encourage students to list prayer needs for others in their books so they can pray for one another during the week. Assign a student coordinator in each small group to gather the group's requests and email them to the group members.

Prayer Connection:

This is the time to encourage, support, and pray for each other as you seek to be know God and submit to His authority.

Share prayer needs with the group, especially those related to submitting to God authority and will. Your group facilitator will close your time in prayer.

Prayer Needs:

Encourage students
to dig a little deeper
y completing a "Now
What" assignment
ore the next time you
eet. Remind students
bout the "Get Ready"
hort daily Bible read-
gs and related ques-
s at the beginning of
Session 8.

now What?

Take it to the next level by completing one of these assignments this week:

Option #1:

Write notes of appreciation to the adult authorities that God has placed in your life. Thank your teacher, coach, or boss for investing in you. Express appreciation for the things you are learning under their influence. Consider writing a similar note to your parents. (You'll give them a wonderful shock!)

Option #2:

Plan to spend time with the Lord each day. Use the time to talk to God through prayer, and learn about His plans for your life through reading Scripture and medi-tating on it. Ask another person to help keep you accountable. Specifically ask God to help you submit to His authority and to the others He has placed in your life.

Bible Reference Notes

Use these notes to deepen your understanding as you study the Bible on your own:

Genesis 2:15
work … take care. Work was part of God's plan from the beginning. Man was given the responsibil of being an obedient servant and wise steward.

Genesis 2:16
any tree. God gave Adam the freedom to choose which tree he would eat from. This included the tree life mentioned in Genesis 2:9.

Genesis 2:17
tree of the knowledge of good and evil. This tree was placed in the garden to give Adam and Eve t opportunity to exercise their freedom of choice. Every tree was appealing, but only one was off limits This "tree" gave them the opportunity to express their obedience and trust in God. The presence of e was not in the substance of the fruit itself. They sinned in their attempt to gain God's knowledge inc pendently of Him.
surely die. Disobeying God results in spiritual death and ultimately physical death. The eating of th forbidden fruit in itself would not result in death. The act of disobedience to God that prompted taki the fruit brought death.

Genesis 3:1
the serpent. While Satan is not referred to in this story, Revelation 12:9 and 20:2 identify Satan wit serpent.

Genesis 3:3
the tree that is in the middle of the garden. This was the tree of the knowledge of good and evil (G 2:9,17). Popular depictions show it as an apple tree, but Scripture does not identify it with any know fruit. Why was the tree there if God did not want them to eat of it? Perhaps because God wanted pec to have a choice about whether to obey Him or not.
or you will die. The clear implication is that God did not originally intend people to have to experien even physical death. Physical death came as a result of human sin (see Rom. 5:12–14).

Genesis 3:5
you will be like God. This is the basis of much of the temptation we face—that we try to be like Go Specific situations in the Bible where this was the case include the Tower of Babel (Gen. 11:1–9), G answer to Job (Job 40:6–41:34), and Christ's third temptation (Matt. 4:8–9). And a prime example is Lucifer's (Satan's) rebellion in heaven that caused him to be cast out of God's presence (Isa. 14:12–

NOTES

NOTES

Session

8

SOLVING THE MAZE

Connections Prep

MAIN LIFEPOINT: Regularly reading and studying the Bible reveals promises, principles, and truths for making critical decisions.

To reinforce the LifePoint, leaders and small-group facilitators should understand the following more detailed CheckPoints and "Do" Points.

BIBLE STUDY CHECKPOINTS:
- Show how studying the Bible can help in making critical decisions
- Demonstrate a working knowledge of how to effectively read and study Scripture
- Explain the importance of applying biblical truths to our decisions

LIFE CHANGE "DO" POINTS:
- Take worship and Bible study notes
- Make a plan to regularly read and study Scripture
- Keep a journal of what you are learning from the Bible

PREPARATION:
- ☐ Review the *Leader's Book* for this session and prepare your teaching.
- ☐ Determine how you will subdivide students into small discussion groups.
- ☐ Recruit mature students or adults as small-group facilitators. Be sure these facilitators plan to attend.
- ☐ Provide a kitchen timer that ticks loudly.
- ☐ Provide a hand or makeup mirror.
- ☐ Provide a Bible.

REQUIRED SUPPLIES:
- ☐ *Critical Decisions: Clarity in the Journey* leader book for each group facilitator
- ☐ *Critical Decisions: Clarity in the Journey* student book for each student
- ☐ Pen or pencil for each student
- ☐ Kitchen timer
- ☐ Makeup mirror
- ☐ Bible

This "Get Ready" section is primarily for the students, but leaders & facilitators will benefit from these devotionals as well.

Get Ready

Spend a few moments getting to know God. Read one of these brief passages each day, and be sure to write down anything He reveals to you.

MONDAY

Read Psalm 19:7-8

What practical benefits have you experienced from knowing the promises of Scripture? How does knowing God's Word change the way you look at the world?

TUESDAY

Read Psalm 19:9-10

How does your daily routine indicate the value you place on the Bible? Could you honestly say that you love God's Word? If so, how do you show it?

WEDNESDAY

Read Psalm 19:11

Have you ever read something in the Bible that helped you through hardship? W are some rewards of following God's instructions?

THURSDAY

Read James 1:22

What does it take to move you to action? Have you ever been deceived? Think ab the impact of being deceived had on you. How did it make you feel?

FRIDAY

Read James 1:23

Who do you see when you look in the mirror? Are you content to hear God's commands without changing your life or personally getting involved in ministry?

SATURDAY

Read James 1:24

Can you remember the last compliment you received? What do you think people would say is the best thing about you? Are you a person of your word or God's Word?

SUNDAY

Read James 1:25

Is it painful to take an honest look at yourself? When you look closely at yourself, what do you see? How likely are you to do whatever it takes to be more like God?

LARGE-GROUP OPENING:
everyone's attention. ake announcements. en your session with a prayer. Read the Point to the students.

Ask students to share out last week's "Now What?" options. Ask em to share to whom they wrote notes of reciation. Did any of em write to their par- ? Ask how their daily e with God has gone s week. Did they ask other person to help p them accountable?

 LifePoint

8

Regularly reading and studying the Bible reveals promises, principles, and truths for making critical decisions.

Say What? *(15 MINUTES)*

Random Question of the Week:
If you could live on another planet, which would you choose?

Group Experience: What Time Is It?

(Permission is granted to copy only this page for use by facilitators as part of t■ Life Connections® Youth Clarity in the Journey study.)

Place the kitchen timer on the floor and turn it on. Ask students to draw six circ■ of equal size on the inside covers of their books. Tell them that the circles repre■ sent clock faces and that they will use a short line (hour hand) and a longer lin■ (minute hand) on each clock face to indicate how much time they spend perforr■ certain daily tasks. Ask them to indicate how much time they spend each day (1■ sleeping, (2) eating, (3) attending school and school work, (4) practicing and p■ ing a sport, instrument, or other interest, (5) watching TV or playing video game■ (5) and reading and studying the Bible. As students work, point out that the tic■ clock is running, signaling they must hurry. (The drawing exercise should not ta■ more than six minutes.)

1. How do you spend most of your time each day?

2. Did the ticking clock help to focus or distract you?

3. How do your drawings represent the decisions you make regarding how you spend your time?

4. How does the time you spend reading and studying your Bible compare with t■ time you spend on other activities? What, if anything, will you do about it?

So What? *(30 MINUTES)*

RGE-GROUP TIME:
ve the students turn
ce the front for this
ching time. Be sure
can make eye con-
t with each student
he room. Encourage
students to follow
g and take notes in
heir *Student Books*.

are the "So What?"
formation with your
e group of students.
u may modify it with
ur own perspectives
and teaching needs.
sure to highlight the
erlined information,
which gives answers
to the *Student Book*
uestions and fill-in-
he-blanks (shown in
your margins).

Teaching Outline

I. Learn the Rules
A. The Bible is like a playbook for life

B. Many people know about the Bible

C. Few people apply the truths of the Bible to their lives

II. Learning from the Bible (Scripture)

III. Just Do It
A. Reading and studying God's Word will help you to avoid wasting your life

B. You will experience freedom from reading and studying the Bible

C. You will bear spiritual fruit when you remain in God's Word

IV. Three Ways to Get the Maximum Benefit from God's Word
A. Study

B. Memorize

C. Apply

V. A Three-Step Process for Applying God's Word
A. Understand what Scriptures meant to the original audience

B. Identify the timeless truth

C. Ask God to show you how to apply the truth to your life

8

EACHING FOR THE
LARGE GROUP:

Learn the Rules

Using the football illustration from a past session, let's consider how a team prepares to play their best and win the game. Most football teams develop a playbook
that contains the plays they plan to use against their opponents. (This language
should sound familiar. Remember the session about the defensive "full armor of
God" and that one offensive weapon—the Sword of the Spirit?) The plays in the
playbook are those a team feels will give them the greatest chance of success. As
coaches develop plays for their teams, they take into account a team's strengths
and weaknesses in the face of their opposition. Because that knowledge is so critical, one of the first things new players have to do is learn the team's playbook. As

a Christian—whether you are new or have been maturing in your faith for some time—you should have a similar priority.

❶ <u>Many people know about the Bible, but fewer actually know the truths it proclaims. Even fewer apply the truths of Scripture to their lives. In fact, they think they would do just as well to read a magazine as to read God's Word.</u> Toda session will help you understand the importance of *applying* God's Word to your decisions.

Learning from the Bible

❶ Why isn't the Bible lived out in the lives of more people?

Learning from the Bible ...

James 1:22-25

Hold up a mirror, using it as a prop as you read the Scripture.

²² But be doers of the word and not hearers only, deceiving yourselves. ²³ Because if one is a hearer of the word and not a doer, he is like a man looking at his own face in mirror; ²⁴ for he looks at himself, goes away, and right away forgets what kind of ma was. ²⁵ But the one who looks intently into the perfect law of freedom and perseveres it, and is not a forgetful hearer but a doer who acts—this person will be blessed in w he does.

Just Do It

James wrote his letter in response to those who claimed Christ as Lord but did n live for Him. How would you feel if soon after your brother died someone said tha they knew and loved him dearly, but acted as if they'd never met Him and knew nothing about Him? That was exactly what James faced.

James was the half-brother of Jesus. His letter was about being a true follower of Christ—not only in what you say, but also in how you live. James wrote about Jesus—the man whom he truly believed to be God's Son. The focus of James' let is on doing what the Bible teaches us to do, not just knowing what the Bible gui us to do. James 1:22-25 shares *why* you should connect to God's Word and provi tips on *how* to connect it to your life. James presents three advantages of readin and studying the Bible.

❷ <u>(1) First, reading and studying God's Word helps you make the most of your life instead of wasting it.</u> James writes, "But be doers of the word and not heare only, deceiving yourselves" (v. 22). James warns about being a casual listener to God's Word. Do you consider simply attending worship enough? Do you sit in wor ship—sometimes even without a Bible—and listen to the sermon, believing tha once or twice a week of "sitting and soaking" is enough to get you by? James di not condone sitting on the back row during sermons, casually making Chinese paper art and passing notes to friends. Instead, James encouraged his audience respect God's Word, to soak it up, and to take it to heart. You must believe in Go

LARGE-GROUP TIME CONTINUED:
This is the meat of the teaching time. Remind students to follow along and take notes in their *Student Books.*

As you share the "So What?" information with students, make it your own.

Emphasize <u>underlined information</u>, which gives key points, answers to the *Student Book* questions or fill-in-the-blanks in the (shown in your margins).

❷ List three advan-tages to reading and studying God's Word.
1.
2.
3.

Word so much that you love to read and hear it, that you delight in daily living it out by faith. If all you do is listen but fail to do what God's Word says, then you are wasting your time. God's Word holds the answers for how you can make the most of your life. That isn't something to take lightly.

❷ (2) Your freedom is a second advantage to reading and studying God's. James describes Scripture as "the perfect law of freedom" (v. 25). The spiritual, moral, and ethical teaching found in the Bible does not restrict you; instead, it offers you greater joy and freedom. Jesus told His disciples that if they followed His teaching they would know the truth and be set free by it (See John 8:31-32). When you try to live the way you think you should instead of the way Scripture tells you to, you become a slave to wondering if you are making the right decisions and suffering when you don't. Life is best when it follows the path that Scripture lays out.

❷ (3) A third advantage to reading and studying God's Word is that you will bear spiritual fruit when you follow its teachings. James says that "the one who looks intently into the perfect law of freedom and perseveres in it, and is not a forgetful hearer but a doer who acts—this person will be blessed in what he does" (v. 25). You will bear spiritual fruits, like peace and love, when you keep your heart open and receptive to Christ, your source of life. Jesus called Himself the vine and you a branch. When you stay connected to Him, your life will bear pleasant things that will bless you and others. But if you are separated from the vine, you will miss out (see John 15.) Your life must be daily grounded in God's Word for you to accomplish the greatness He has planned for you.

Three Ways to Get the Maximum Benefit from God's Word

In addition to supplying the advantages of reading and studying the Bible, James offers instruction in how to get the best of the best God gives you. ❸ (1)First, James says that you are to study Scripture carefully. He says the person who will benefit from God's Word is "the one who looks intently into [it]" (v. 25). Studying the Bible means taking time to understand the text's original meaning. That means asking the right questions. You don't need to be a preacher or Bible scholar. In fact, the vast majority of Christians are not professionally trained in the Bible. However, anyone can learn scriptural basics such as who wrote each biblical book, when each was written, what the customs and culture of the time were, and who the intended readers were. You can find much of this information in a good study Bible or commentary. As you gain insight into what you are reading, write it in the margins of your Bible.

❸ (2)James also says to memorize. He writes that the man who enjoys the benefits of Scripture "is not a forgetful hearer" (v. 25). Among the things you have

❸ In order to experience the full benefit of cripture you must …

Read, reread, and listen to it.

Analyze, ponder, and pick it apart.

Study, memorize, and apply it to your life.

8

memorized to date are your address, phone number, birthdays, song lyrics, jokes sports statistics, your multiplication tables, and the route between home and school. You can memorize whatever you put your mind to. Psalm 119:11 says, "I have treasured Your word in my heart so that I may not sin against You." To "treasure" God's Word is memorize it. Scripture sheds light on the decisions you need to make. God's revealed Word will illuminate the path to making critical decision Memorizing verses gives us the truths we need to navigate life, and it prepares for opportunities to share Christ with others.

❸ (3)The third means of gaining maximum benefit from God's Word is to apply daily to your life. If you could sum up the theme of James in one word, it would b "do." If you *do* apply God's Word to your life, you "will be blessed" in what you *d* (v. 25).

A Three-Step Process for Applying God's Word

❹ Applying Scripture is a three-step process. (1) First, you must understand wha passage meant to the original audience. To do this, you must study the backgroun of the passage. (2) Secondly, you should try to identify the timeless truth a sectio holds. What is it about a passage's teaching that holds true for all people, in all places, at all times? (3) Third, you must ask God to show you how to apply that ti less truth to your own life. Understanding apart from the Holy Spirit isn't possible.

❹ **List the three steps to applying Scripture.**
1. Understand what the Scripture meant to the original audience.
2. Identify the timeless truth.
3. Ask God to show you how to apply the timeless truth to your life.

Do What? *(15 MINUTES)*

Group Experience: Grasping God's Word

Hold the Bible in your hand, and point out that you are "grasping" God's Word. Ask students to provide other definitions for the word "grasp." (For example, "to hold on to, to understand.") Hold the Bible loosely between your thumb and index finger, and allow a student to pull the Bible out of your hand. Now hold your Bible firmly by wrapping all your fingers around it. Ask another student to try to pull the Bible from your grasp, but do not let him. Point out that having a firm grasp on God's Word will help us survive in this journey called life. Use your thumb and fingers to illustrate this principle of grasping God's Word:

1. Hearing God's Word (thumb)

2. Reading God's Word (index finger)

3. Studying God's Word (middle finger)

4. Memorizing God's Word (ring finger)

5. Meditating on God's Word (pinky finger)

6. Doing what God's Word Says (palm)

Discuss with students that each of these disciplines is essential to truly grasping God's Word. Discuss opportunities students might have to experience each of the six ways of understanding Scripture. For example, you can hear God's Word at church, on television, and through Christian music.

Small-group facilitators should reinforce the LifePoint for this session. Make sure that student's questions are invited and addressed honestly.

↗ LifePoint Review

Regularly reading and studying the Bible reveals promises, principles, and truths for making critical decisions.

"Do" Points:

These "Do" Points will help you grab hold of this week's LifePoint. Be open and honest as you answer the questions within your small group.

1. <u>Worship service is only one place where you can hear the Word of God.</u> Other places may include Bible study or small accountability group. You may also he the Word of God through some music.
   How might taking notes on worship and Bible reading benefit you?

2. <u>Make a plan to regularly read and study Scripture.</u> The Bible is full of poetry, history, adventure, bravery, and so much more! Best of all, it offers guidelines for living.
   Can you make a commitment to read the Bible every day? If so, what's you action plan?

3. <u>Keep a journal of what you are learning from the Bible.</u> Journaling is a great w to better understand what you are reading. It can help you make connections between the words of Scripture and the things going on in your life.
   Have you ever kept a personal diary at home or a journal for a class? Will y begin one to record what God is telling you through His Word?

Be sure to end your session by asking students to share prayer needs with one another, especially as they relate to issues brought up by today's session.

Encourage students to list prayer needs for others in their books so they can pray for one another during the week. Assign a student coordinator in each small group to gather the group's requests and e-mail them to the group members.

Prayer Connection:

This is the time to encourage, support, and pray for each other as you read and study the Bible to discover tools for godly living.

Share prayer needs with the group, especially those related to personal Bible stu Your group facilitator will close your time in prayer.

Prayer Needs:

now What?

Encourage students to dig a little deeper completing a "Now What" assignment before the next time u meet. Remind students about the "Get dy" short daily Bible readings and related estions at the beginning of Session 9.

Take it to the next level by completing one of these assignments this week:

Option #1:
Consider the "Do What?" activity, "Grasping God's Word." Research the Bible to find out more about the six disciplines to better understanding Scripture. Hint: Psalm 119:11 can be used to support one of them. Trace the outline of your hand on a sheet of paper, and label your fingers and palm with the corresponding Scripture references.

Option #2:
Create your own sermon-notes notebook. Fill a small binder with paper, and begin taking notes on each Sunday's sermon. At the top of each page, list the date, the name of the person preaching, the topic, and the Scripture references cited. As you listen to God's Word being preached, take notes.

8

Bible Reference Notes

Use these notes to deepen your understanding as you study the Bible on your own:

James 1:22

merely listen. The Christian must not just hear the Word of God. A response is required.
deceive yourselves. To make mere knowledge of God's will the sole criterion for the religious life is gerous and self-deceptive.
Do what it says. This is James' main point in this section.

James 1:23-24

James illustrates his point with a metaphor. The person who reads Scripture (which is a mirror to th Christian, because in it his or her true state is shown), and then goes away unchanged is like the person who gets up in the morning and sees how dirty and disheveled he or she is, but then prompt forgets about it (when the proper response would be to get cleaned up).

James 1:25

the perfect law. The reference is probably to the teachings of Jesus that set one free, in contrast to Jewish law, which brought bondage (see Rom. 8:2).
continues. Such people make obedience to the gospel a continuing part of their lives.
blessed. The sheer act of keeping this law is a happy experience in and of itself because it produce good fruit, now and in the future.

Session

9

REFLECTING CHRIST THROUGH THE JOURNEY

Connections Prep

MAIN LIFEPOINT: Guiding the believer to live in such a way as to reflect Christ in all areas, the Holy Spirit is God's personal presence with us.

To reinforce the LifePoint, leaders and small group facilitators should understand the following more detailed CheckPoints and "Do" Points.

BIBLE STUDY CHECKPOINTS:
- Explain the role of the Holy Spirit
- Give reasons why we should follow the Holy Spirit's guidance
- Learn to recognize how the Holy Spirit aids in making critical decisions

LIFE CHANGE "DO" POINTS:
- Listen for the Holy Spirit's promptings
- Keep a journal of the Holy Spirit's activity in your life
- Pray that God will give you peace in making decisions

PREPARATION:
- ☐ Review the *Leader's Book* for this session and prepare your teaching.
- ☐ Determine how you will subdivide students into small discussion groups.
- ☐ Recruit mature students or adults as small-group facilitators. Be sure these facilitators plan to attend.
- ☐ A blindfold for every student.
- ☐ Prerecord or provide an audio version of John 16:5-16.
- ☐ Set up an audio player.
- ☐ Find a sound effects CD.

REQUIRED SUPPLIES:
- ☐ *Critical Decisions: Clarity in the Journey* leader books for each group facilitator
- ☐ *Critical Decisions: Clarity in the Journey* student books for each student
- ☐ Pen or pencil for each student
- ☐ Blindfolds for each student
- ☐ A CD player
- ☐ A sound effects CD

 Get Ready

Spend a few moments getting to know God. Read one of these brief passages each day, and be sure to write down anything He reveals to you.

MONDAY

Read John 16:5-6

What is your first reaction when a trusted and good friend is removed from your life? Do you feel abandoned? Do you question God? If you were able to see everything—past, present, and future—at once, how would it change the way you feel?

TUESDAY

Read John 16:7-8

Would you be willing to give up the best thing you've ever had for the promise of something even better? Think about what might be better than "the best thing you've ever had." How easily would you put faith in that kind of promise?

WEDNESDAY

Read John 16:9

Do you understand "sin" as a list of things in your life, or an alien force that co-exists with who you really are? What is the difference? What does the differen mean to you right now?

THURSDAY

Read John 16:10

Would you have liked to personally know Jesus when He walked the earth? If you had been His friend during that time, do you think doing the right thing would ha been easier or more difficult than it is now? Why?

FRIDAY

Read John 16:11

Are you judgmental? Is it ever all right to pass judgment on something evil? By what standard do you judge right and wrong?

SATURDAY

Read John 16:12-13

When is enough, enough? Is it possible for anything to be too good? Can you handle the truth? Ask God what it means to be guided into "all truth."

SUNDAY

Read John 16:14-16

What do you consider the most reliable method of delivering a message? Would you trust a singing telegram? What is the best news you've ever received?

9

LARGE-GROUP OPENING:
t everyone's attention.
Make announcements.
pen your session with
a prayer. Read the
ePoint to the students.

Ask for a volunteer to
hare his or her experi-
ces with last session's
Now What?" activities.

 LifePoint

Guiding the believer to live in such a way as to reflect Christ in all areas, the Holy Spirit is God's personal presence with us.

SMALL-GROUP TIME:
Instruct students to separate into smaller groups of 4-8, preferably in a circle configuration. Call on the mature student or adult leaders you recruited to facilitate each small group through this "Say What?" segment.

Say What? *(15 MINUTES)*

Random Question of the Week:

What makes tomatoes fruits instead of vegetables?

Group Experience: Blind Simon Says

(Permission is granted to copy only this page for use by facilitators as part of the Life Connections® Youth Clarity in the Journey study.)

Ask students to put on their blindfolds. Then lead them in a game of "Simon Say Tell them to stand up, sit down, stand on one foot, wave their right hands, and so on. If anyone misses a Simon-direction, ask them to sit down. At the conclusion o the game, tell students to take off their blindfolds and discuss how it felt to play the familiar game while blindfolded.

1. How did the blindfold affect the way you played the game?

2. Were you more concerned about yourself or the other players?

3. How do you know that everyone was playing fair?

4. How do you know that you were not the only one blindfolded?

5. How is playing "Blind Simon Says" like following the Holy Spirit's direction in your life?

RGE-GROUP TIME:
ve the students turn
ace the front for this
aching time. Be sure
 can make eye con-
ct with each student
the room. Encourage
students to follow
ng and take notes in
their *Student Books.*

So What? *(30 MINUTES)*

Teaching Outline

I. The Voices You Hear
A. There are many voices in life
B. You are called to follow God's voice

II. Learning from the Bible (Scripture)

III. The Holy Spirit's Role in the World
A. Shows the need for God
B. Presents Jesus as the Way
C. Reminds you how God feels about sin

IV. The Holy Spirit's Personal Presence in Your Life
A. The Spirit guides you
B. The Spirit can be trusted
C. The Spirit speaks the Words of God

V. Sensing the Spirit's Presence in Your Life
A. You feel peace
B. You will be convicted in your decision making

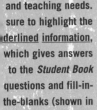

TEACHING FOR THE
LARGE GROUP:
hare the "So What?"
information with your
ge group of students.
ju may modify it with
our own perspectives
and teaching needs.
sure to highlight the
derlined information,
which gives answers
to the *Student Book*
questions and fill-in-
the-blanks (shown in
your margins).

9

The Voices You Hear

Hearing voices is a good thing. It means your ears are working well. But if you start hearing voices when no one else is around, well, that can be a problem. In fact, it would probably be better if you didn't let your friends know about your hidden talent.

Wearing an earpiece, however, changes everything. If you are wearing an earpiece or headphone from your iPod, you can hear or even dance to voices without questions or strange looks.

❶ What are three of the Holy Spirit's functions?

❷ What has the Lord called you to do?

Learning from the Bible ...

John 16:5-16

Prerecord the following Scripture, using someone's voice that students may not easily recognize. You may choose to provide a commercial audio recording of the verse instead. Play the audio, and then ask students if they recognized the voice.

Today's lesson is about ❶ the Holy Spirit who functions as an invisible earpiece, prompting us to honor God, reminding us of what God's Word says, and quietly encouraging us to stay on track with Him. ❷ The Lord has called you to follow H voice and carry out His instructions. In today's session you will learn how the Hol Spirit guides you in every area of life, and you will learn how to tune in to His gentle voice.

Learning from the Bible

⁵ *"But now I am going away to Him who sent Me, and not one of you asks Me, 'Where a You going?' ⁶Yet, because I have spoken these things to you, sorrow has filled your hea ⁷Nevertheless, I am telling you the truth. It is for your benefit that I go away, because I don't go away the Counselor will not come to you. If I go, I will send Him to you. ⁸Whe He comes, He will convict the world about sin, righteousness, and judgment: ⁹about sin because they do not believe in Me; ¹⁰about righteousness, because I am going to the Father and you will no longer see Me; ¹¹and about judgment, because the ruler of this world has been judged.*

¹²"I still have many things to tell you, but you can't bear them now. ¹³When the Spirit o truth comes, He will guide you into all the truth. For He will not speak on His own, but He will speak whatever He hears. He will also declare to you what is to come. ¹⁴He will glorify Me, because He will take from what is Mine and declare it to you. ¹⁵Everything t Father has is Mine. This is why I told you that He takes from what is Mine and will decl it to you.

¹⁶"A little while and you will no longer see Me; again a little while and you will see Me.

The Holy Spirit's Role in the World

As Jesus prepared to go to the cross, He wanted His disciples to know that He would not leave them alone in the world. In John 16:5-16, Jesus gave them encou agement that also applies to us: "It is for your benefit that I go away, because if don't go away the Counselor will not come to you. If I go, I will send Him to you" (v. 7). "When He comes," Jesus said, "He will convict the world about sin, righteou ness, and judgment: about sin, because they do not believe in Me" (vv.8-9).

❸ List three functions of the Holy Spirit.
1. He helps you recognize your need for God.
2. He proclaims that Christ is the answer to your separation from God.
3. He reminds the world of God's attitude toward sin.

❸ The Holy Spirit serves three primary functions. (1)First, He helps us recognize our need for God, convincing those who are not yet believers of their need for a relationship with God. Furthermore, (2) the Holy Spirit serves as that wonderfully nagging feeling that leads people to see that Jesus Christ is the only way to recon nect with their Creator. (3) Third, the Spirit reminds the world of God's attitude toward sin. He prompts us to consider the consequences of disobeying God's Word

ARGE-GROUP TIME
CONTINUED:
his is the meat of the
aching time. Remind
dents to follow along
nd take notes in their
Student Books.

As you share the
o What?" information
with students, make
it your own. Use your
atural teaching style.

mphasize underlined
rmation, which gives
ey points, answers to
the *Student Book*
uestions or fill-in-the-
anks in the (shown in
your margins).

❹ In the same way
us taught and guided
e disciples, the Spirit
ntinues to teach and
ide those who follow
Christ.

❺ On whose
authority does the
Holy Spirit speak?

When you hear God's voice in your life you have a choice. You can choose to ignore the promptings of the Holy Spirit or you can listen to God's voice and follow the Spirit. In both Hebrews 3:7-8 and 15 you are warned, "Today, if you hear His voice, do not harden your heart(s)." Each time you fail to recognize or refuse to follow the Spirit's voice in your life, your heart will grow harder. As your heart becomes harder you hear God's voice less and less and move farther away from His will for your life. You begin to make decisions that are inconsistent with how He created you. You become convinced that neither your parents nor anyone else God has placed in your life are as smart as you.

Take just a moment, indulge yourself, and mentally get into that car of your dreams for the first time and drive down a familiar road. Now look out the window—quickly, since you are driving. What do you see? Everything looks different. The same roads you have traveled for years in the backseat of your parent's car and riding shotgun with friends looks surprisingly new. The landmarks and billboards seem more significant. They seem like they are directed to you. When you put your trust in God and listen to His Spirit you begin to notice Him working all around you. You begin to hear God's voice prompting you.

The Holy Spirit's Personal Presence in Your Life

❹ In the same way Jesus taught and guided the disciples, the Spirit continues to teach and guide those who follow Christ. But it's important to recognize that while the Holy Spirit wants to guide you, He will not force Himself on you. The Spirit will control your thoughts and actions only to the point that you allow Him. As you make decisions about how to react in a relationship or how to be a person on integrity in a challenging situation, the Spirit is present to help you make the right choices. He does not, however, make them for you.

It's encouraging to know that the Holy Spirit can always be trusted. Jesus said, "When the Spirit of truth comes, He will guide you into all the truth" (v. 13). Remember, ❺ the Holy Spirit speaks the words of your Heavenly Father who cares deeply for you: "He will not speak on His own, but He will speak whatever He hears" (v. 13). The Spirit will whisper God's direction for you into your heart and mind. Similar to your conscience, He will convict you about right and wrong. He will also encourage you to view your life through God's eyes—as a string of opportunities to live for Him and to bless others.

When you put your trust in God and listen to His Spirit, you begin to notice Him working all around you. You become more sensitive to doing what He wants you to do. You become more determined to follow what His Word teaches.

117

6 True or False:
The Holy Spirit uses
Scripture, godly coun-
sel, and prayer to com-
municate to you. (True)

7 How can you sense
the Holy Spirit's
guidance?

6 <u>The Holy Spirit uses Scripture, godly counsel, and prayer to communicate to y</u>
He also guides you through the internal promptings as we've discussed. It's imp
tant to recognize that the Holy Spirit is not an IV that you must wait to have inse
ed into your spiritual veins. He is not a fog that will descend on you as you sleep
7 <u>When you accept Jesus into your life, the Holy Spirit comes too. And from that</u>
<u>moment on, you'll be able to sense His guidance through the peace He gives you</u>

The Spirit will convict you of sin. He will bring the truths of Scripture when you a
faced with tough situations. He will fill your mind with godly knowledge. He is a
faithful and capable Counselor.

SMALL-GROUP TIME:
Use this time to help
students begin to inte-
grate the truth they've
learned into their lives
while they connect with
other students in the
group, the leaders, and
with God.

After presenting the
teaching material, ask
students to divide back
into small groups and
discuss the "Do What?"
questions. Small group
facilitators should lead
the discussions and set
they tone by being open
and honest in respond-
ing to each question.

 # Do What? *(15 MINUTES)*

Group Experience: Too Much Noise

Set up a CD player with a CD of sound effects. Play a quick round of "Name that
Sound Effect," allowing the boys to compete against the girls. Recognize the nu
ber of sound effects correctly identified.

1. Name some of the good noises in the world. Then list some of the bad.

2. The world is full of so much noise that it is sometimes difficult to hear God's
   voice. What do you need to do in order to hear God?
   - ☐ Turn your music down
   - ☐ Read the Bible more
   - ☐ Stop watching TV
   - ☐ Spend less time with friends
   - ☐ Memorize Scripture
   - ☐ Play video games less
   - ☐ Wake up earlier and spend some quiet time with God
   - ☐ Spend the last minutes of your day with God
   - ☐ Pray more often

3. Jesus says, "My sheep hear my voice, I know them, and they follow Me" (John 10:27). How have you most recently been aware of Jesus' voice? What did you feel His Spirit prompting you to do?

hall-group facilitators should reinforce the LifePoint for this session, make sure that udent's questions are nvited and addressed honestly.

 # LifePoint Review

Guiding the believer to live in such a way as to reflect Christ in all areas, the Holy Spirit is God's personal presence with us.

"Do" Points:

These "Do" Points will help you grab hold of this week's LifePoint. Be open and honest as you answer the questions within your small group.

1. <u>Listen for the Spirit's promptings.</u> God speaks to you through your conscience and the peace—or lack of it— that you feel.
   What is the Holy Spirit telling you to do?

2. <u>Keep a journal of the Holy Spirit's activity in your life.</u> Whether you realize it or not, God is always working in and around you.
   Are you able to easily identify the Holy Spirit's work in your life? How can you tell if God is working in you or if you're trying to do things in your own power?

3. <u>Pray that God will give you peace in making decisions.</u> Every day you are force
make decisions. Some are easy. Others require prayerful consideration.
What decision faces you that requires God's help? How likely are you to follow His counsel?

Be sure to end your session by asking students to share prayer needs with one another, especially as they relate to issues brought up by today's session.

Encourage students to list prayer needs for others in their books so they can pray for one another during the week. Assign a student coordinator in each small group to gather the group's requests and e-mail them to the group members.

Prayer Connection:

This is the time to encourage, support, and pray for each other as you trust the I
Spirit to guide you in how to live for Christ.

Share prayer needs with the group, especially those related to hearing from and responding to God. Close the time in prayer.

Prayer Needs:

Encourage students to dig a little deeper completing a "Now What?" assignment re the next time you et. Remind students out the "Get Ready" ort daily Bible readgs and related quesons at the beginning Session 10.

 # now What?

Take it to the next level by completing one of these assignments this week:

Option #1:
Spend 15 minutes each day reading your Bible in a quiet place. Begin your time with a simple prayer, asking God to open your heart and mind to His Will. Do not ask for anything else. As you spend time meditating on Scripture, keep a journal nearby. As the Holy Spirit prompts you, record what He brings to mind.

Option #2:
List three decisions you face this week. Keep the list in your Bible and refer to it at least twice a day. Every time you read it, pray that the Holy Spirit will guide you to do the make the right decisions—decisions that honor God.

9

Bible Reference Notes

Use these notes to deepen your understanding as you study the Bible on your own:

John 16:5

none of you asks. Peter did ask this question in John 13:36: "Lord, where are you going?" and Jesus replied: "Where I am going, you cannot follow now, but you will follow later." Some commentators se this as evidence that chapters 13–16 are a compilation of several teachings of Jesus arranged in th format to give a summary of Jesus' teaching to believers. Others think that Jesus is responding to th fact that Peter didn't understand the significance of the answer Jesus gave to Peter's question.

John 16:7

It is for your good that I am going away. Jesus' departure meant the coming of the Counselor. The Greek term used for the Holy Spirit is *paraclete*. It is a rich term for which there is no adequate Engl translation. Attempts such as Counselor or Helper or Comforter fail because they emphasize only on many aspects of the term. Jesus is telling the disciples that He will return to them in a deep, inner, itual way. He had also referred to the Spirit in John 7:38–39: "Whoever believes in me, as the Script has said, streams of living water will flow from within him." By this He meant the Spirit, whom thos who believed in Him were later to receive. Up to that time the Spirit had not been given, since Jesus not yet been glorified (see also John 14:15–18).

John 16:8

he will convict the world of guilt in regard to sin and righteousness and judgment. The "world" he that Jesus was an unrighteous sinner under the judgment of God (John 9:24). The Spirit will prove th the world is wrong about its convictions on these matters. "Righteousness" (perhaps better transla as "justice") is shown by the Father's vindication of Jesus through His resurrection and ascension (v. 10).

John 16:13

He will not speak on his own. Jesus only speaks the words of His Father; the Spirit only speaks the words of Jesus. Each member of the Trinity seeks the glory and honor of the other (see John 8:54; 12 16:14; 17:1,4–5).

John 16:15

All that belongs to the Father is mine ... the Spirit will ... make it known to you. The incredible tru of the gospel is that God has fully revealed Himself to His people. Even believers who never saw Jesu physically are not at a disadvantage compared to those who did, for the Spirit continually reveals Je and the Father to whomever comes in faith to Christ.

John 16:16

In a little while ... then after a little while. This riddle may be intentionally ambiguous. Does the fir "little while" mean after His resurrection or after His return in glory? Does "seeing" mean physical s or spiritual sight—as it so often does in this Gospel? If the latter, then the second "little while" ma mean His coming to them by His Spirit (John 14:18–20). It would not be unlike this author to mean the above!

Session

10

OBSTACLES ALONG THE WAY

Connections Prep

MAIN LIFEPOINT:
God uses everything we experience—even the most difficult circumstances—to accomplish His will and form our character for navigating the critical path.

To reinforce the LifePoint, leaders and small group facilitators should understand the following more detailed CheckPoints and "Do" Points.

BIBLE STUDY CHECKPOINTS:
· Understand how God uses the circumstances in our lives
· Explain how we should deal with difficult circumstances
· Understand how Joseph trusted God through adversity

LIFE CHANGE "DO" POINTS:
· Spend time with Christians whose faith has matured through adversity
· Study biblical accounts of people who experienced great adversity yet discovered God's will for their lives
· Confess bitterness from trials you've experienced to God

PREPARATION:
☐ Review the *Leader's Book* for this session and prepare your teaching.
☐ Determine how you will subdivide students into small discussion groups.
☐ Recruit mature students or adults as small-group facilitators. Be sure these facilitators plan to attend.

REQUIRED SUPPLIES:
☐ *Critical Decisions: Clarity in the Journey* leader books for each group facilitator
☐ *Critical Decisions: Clarity in the Journey* student books for each student
☐ Pen or pencil for each student

10

This "Get Ready"
section is primarily for
the students, but leaders
and facilitators will
benefit from these
devotionals too.

 # Get Ready

*Spend a few moments getting to know God. Read one of these brief
passages each day, and be sure to write down anything He reveals to you*

MONDAY

Read Genesis 45:4-5

Have you ever looked into the eyes of someone you intentionally hurt? What did y
expect that person to say or do? Were you surprised by their words or actions?

TUESDAY

Read Genesis 45:6-11

Who, in addition to your parents, has God placed in your life to take care of you?
How does God speak to you through the care provided?

WEDNESDAY

Read Genesis 50:15

In what do you place your sense of security? If that possession, principle, or pers
were taken away from you, how would it change your outlook on life?

THURSDAY

Read Genesis 50:16-17

What is the worst thing you've ever experienced? How long did it take you to
overcome it? Had you forgotten about it until now?

FRIDAY

Read Genesis 50:18-19

Is there a person in your life that deserves your mercy? Think of ways that you can show mercy to those around you. Why would you decide to do this?

SATURDAY

Read Genesis 50:20

What have you done that turned out exactly the opposite from what you expected? List ways that God can make all things work for the good of those who seek to follow His ways.

SUNDAY

Read Genesis 50:21

When have your words delivered comfort to someone in need? How has someone else's kindness calmed your fears?

LARGE-GROUP OPENING:
everyone's attention. ▌ake announcements. ▌en your session with a prayer. Read the ▌Point to the students.

Ask students to tell ▌out last week's "Now What?" options. Ask them to share about ▌r times with God this ▌eek. Did they receive ▌n answer for at least ▌ne of the three deci- ▌ions they are facing? ▌Were they able make ▌sions that honor God with the Holy Spirit's help?

 LifePoint

10

God uses everything we experience—even the most difficult circumstances— to accomplish His will and form our character for navigating the critical path.

Say What? *(15 MINUTES)*

Random Question of the Week:
What is your favorite gadget?

Group Experience: Worst Case Scenario

(Permission is granted to copy only this page for use by facilitators as part of th
Life Connections® Youth Clarity in the Journey study.)

Read the following aloud:

One morning you get out of bed and slip on the notes you left on the floor the pr
ous night. With a sickening thud, you land on your tailbone—an injury that will
throb for hours. As you are sprawled on the floor in pain, you realize your alarm
not go off. You have only 15 minutes to dress, and you can't find one of your sho

After you settle on a different pair, you realize that your ride must've decided to
stay home sick. You begin frantically punching numbers into the phone in hopes
finding another. But by the time you get to school, you are late with no excuse. A
you head to history class, you realize that in your rush to get to school, you have
forgotten all of your books. Worse, you have an open book test this morning. You
take the test, hoping for a passing grade. No such luck.

Soon, you realize you have no lunch. No lunch money. No one to share his lunch
you or to loan you money to get your own. Finally, after a long day you get home
to realize you are locked out.

1. If this described your day, what would have been the worst part?

2. At what point would you have given up?

3. How could God use a day like this to accomplish His will and mature our
faith in Him?

RGE-GROUP TIME:
ve the students turn
ce the front for this
ching time. Be sure
can make eye con-
t with each student
he room. Encourage
students to follow
g and take notes in
heir *Student Books*.

 # So What? *(30 MINUTES)*

Teaching Outline

I. Bad Things Happen
A. Life is uncertain

B. Your response to life's circumstances determines your level of success

C. The Bible presents Job as someone from whom we can learn about adversity

II. Learning from the Bible (Scripture)

III. Responding to Difficult Circumstances
A. Bad things happen to everyone

B. God can use circumstances to get your attention

C. God can use circumstances to gain your affection

D. God can use circumstances to grow your character

IV. Honoring God Through All Circumstances
A. Joseph refused to blame others

B. Joseph refused to become bitter

C. Joseph recognized God's timing as perfect

EACHING FOR THE
LARGE GROUP:
nare the "So What?"
ching with your stu-
nts. You may modify
it to fit your needs.

sure to highlight the
erlined information,
ch gives answers to
Student Book ques-
tions and fill-in-the-
anks (shown in your
margins).

Bad Things Happen

"Life is like a box of chocolates." Everybody understands this. When you grab a chocolate from the box, are you going to get one of those rich, caramel-filled pieces—or something very close to disgusting (and we've all got our favorites). If you have ever watched not-so-old movie classic television you may have come across *Forrest Gump*, a movie that chronicles the life of a simple southern boy who lives the most amazing life. His life is packed full of heartache (he loses his girl-friend) and triumph (he is a war hero honored by the president). When asked about his life he compares it to a box of chocolates from which we grab pieces by piece.

10

You've been around long enough to realize that there are some really awesome things about life and some that are just plain lousy. That's why you must recog that more important than what happens to you is how you respond to what hap to you. How do you react when you don't get the job, flunk the driving test, or lo friend's trust? Have you observed how others respond when their parents separa their pets die, or their cars break down? Does the way you or others handle hard times seem to affect how things turn out? ❶ How you respond to adversity will determine your level of success in making critical decisions along the way.

A great example of someone who fought successfully through adversity is found the Old Testament. There, in the midst of prosperity and blessings, Job tragicall loses everything he owns. ❷ Yet at the end of the series of terrible circumstanc Job finds more blessings and greater purpose in his life than ever before. The k to his success was Job's response to adversity. At first, Job struggles to find cau and meaning in these terrible circumstances. But by the conclusion of the story God chastises Job's friends for not being as honest as Job while affirming Job fo his response to adversity.

In today's session you will see how another Old Testament figure learned how to relate to God during terrible circumstances. Through his decision to focus on Go when times were bad, God's will for him was accomplished.

Learning from the Bible

[NARRATOR] *4 Then Joseph said to his brothers,*
[JOSEPH] *"Please, come near me,"*
[NARRATOR] *and they came near.*
[JOSEPH] *"I am Joseph, your brother,"*
[NARRATOR] *he said,*
[JOSEPH] *"the one you sold into Egypt. 5 And now don't be worried or angry with yourselves for selling me here, because God sent me ahead of you to preserve life. 6 For the famine has been in the land these two years, and there will be five more ye without plowing or harvesting. 7 God sent me ahead of you to establish you as a remn within the land and to keep you alive by a great deliverance. 8 Therefore it was not y who sent me here, but God. He has made me a father to Pharaoh, lord of his entire household, and ruler over all the land of Egypt.*
9 "Return quickly to my father and say to him, 'This is what your son Joseph says: "G has made me lord of all Egypt. Come down to me without delay. 10 You can settle in t land of Goshen and be near me—you, your children, and grandchildren, your sheep,

---

❶ Your response to the circumstances in your life will determine your level of success in making critical decisions along the way.

❷ What was key to Job's experiencing great blessings after such tragedy?

Learning from the Bible ...

Genesis 45:4-11; 50:15-21

Ask for volunteers to come to the front and read the parts of (1) the narrator, (2) Joseph, and (3) the brothers. Ask three others to come to the front and read the parts of the brothers.

ARGE-GROUP TIME CONTINUED:
his is the meat of the aching time. Remind dents to follow along d take notes in their *Student Books.*

As you share the "What?" information with students, make t your own. Use your atural teaching style.

mphasize underlined rmation, which gives ey points, answers to the *Student Book* estions or fill-in-the- nks in the (shown in your margins).

cattle, and all you have. *¹¹* *There I will sustain you, for there will be five more years of famine. Otherwise, you, your household, and everything you have will become destitute.'"*

[NARRATOR] *¹⁵* *When Joseph's brothers saw that their father was dead, they said to one another,*
[BROTHERS] *"If Joseph is holding a grudge against us, he will certainly repay us for all the wrong we caused him."*
[NARRATOR] *¹⁶* *So they sent this message to Joseph,*
[BROTHERS] *"Before he died your father gave a command: ¹⁷ 'Say this to Joseph: Please forgive your brothers' transgression and their sin—the wrong they caused you.' Therefore, please forgive the transgression of the servants of the God of your father."*
[NARRATOR] *Joseph wept when their message came to him. ¹⁸ Then his brothers also came to him, bowed down before him, and said,*
[BROTHERS] *"We are your slaves!"*
[NARRATOR] *¹⁹ But Joseph said to them,*
[JOSEPH] *"Don't be afraid. Am I in the place of God? ²⁰ You planned evil against me; God planned it for good to bring about the present result—the survival of many people. ²¹ Therefore don't be afraid. I will take care of you and your little ones."*
[NARRATOR] *And he comforted them and spoke kindly to them.*

Responding to Difficult Circumstances

When things don't go your way—even when they fight against you—you can easily start to wonder where God is hiding. You may even doubt His presence in your life and might be tempted to stop believing His promises. It's at that point that your course can be determined. ❸ You may respond to the bad things that happen to you with doubt and a passive posture, or you may respond with a spirit that probes for the deeper things that may come as a result. These are the lessons that stand loyally by you as you make the decisions that plot the course of the your life.

❸ What are the two ays you can choose to respond to adversity?

The choice is illustrated in the following scenario:

10

"A bounty of $5,000 was offered for each wolf captured alive. Sam and Jed saw dollar signs so they became overnight bounty hunters. They scoured the mountains both day and night in search of their fortune. After several days of unsuccessful hunting, they fell asleep from exhaustion. In the middle of the night, Sam suddenly awoke to see that they were surrounded by about fifty wolves with flaming eyes and bared teeth. He nudged his partner, 'Jed, wake up! We're rich!'[1]

[1] *Raymond McHenry, ed. The Best of In Other Words (Houston, TX: Raymond McHenry, 1969), 324.*

❹ Give three ways God can use the circumstances in your life.

God can and will use the circumstances that come your way. ❹ (1) The first step t trusting Him in this is to recognize that God wants to get your attention. ❺ He ma do this through something your parents say, the way He answers your prayers, the amount of time He takes to answer your prayers, through hurt feelings, sickness, blessings, tragedy, good friendships, bad friendships, and anything else He choos God uses different methods, at different times, to get through to different people. example, God used the prophet Nathan's advice to get David's attention—both wh he was a shepherd and when he was a king (2 Samuel 12:1-13). But when Balaa started out in the wrong direction, God grabbed his attention by speaking to him through—yes, it's true—a donkey (Numbers 22:21-34)!

❹ (2) Sometimes God uses circumstances to gain your affection, too. As you lea to depend on God when things get tough, you will love Him more and more—jus you do a friend who is always there when you need her.

❺ Check the methods God may use to get your attention:
- ☐ **Through something your parents say**
- ☐ **Through the way He answers your prayers**
- ☐ **Through the amount of time He takes to answer your prayers**
- ☐ **Through hurt feelings**
- ☐ **Through sickness**
- ☐ **Through blessings**
- ☐ **Through tragedy**
- ☐ **Through good friendships**
- ☐ **Through bad friendships**

❹ (3) It's also important to realize that God uses circumstances to grow your character. As you grow in character, in integrity and wisdom, you become a stror more confident person. You also become more dependable and begin to develop and stick to strong convictions. Having character leads to your becoming more trustworthy. And it's during the tough times that character grows best.

Honoring God in All Circumstances

The people in the Bible struggled with many of the same issues you do today. Joseph, for instance, dealt with and paid the price for his brothers' jealousy. In fac circumstances between Joseph and his brothers grew so bad that the brothers thre him into a pit and sold him as a slave (Genesis 37). Later, after things finally star looking up, Joseph was falsely accused of rape and thrown into prison. But becaus Joseph's commitment to God and God's favor on him, Joseph was eventually freed went on to the position of second in command over all of Egypt.

Joseph could have blamed his brothers for all the bad things that happened to him—especially since they were the direct cause of most of it, but he didn't.

❻ In what three ways did Joseph deal with his circumstances?

❻ (1) He refused to blame others: a key factor in his response to life's difficulti Joseph saw no benefit in pointing fingers at those who hurt him. Instead, he chc to look for God's hand and deeper understanding through his situation.

❻ (2) Furthermore, Joseph refused to become bitter. In Genesis 50, Joseph did n look at the individual snapshots of his life, assigning anger and resentment to t brothers who brought him such hurt. He offered his brothers forgiveness and mu needed food instead. He welcomed them with kind words: "Don't be afraid. Am I

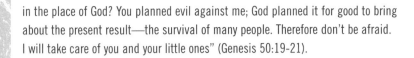

in the place of God? You planned evil against me; God planned it for good to bring about the present result—the survival of many people. Therefore don't be afraid. I will take care of you and your little ones" (Genesis 50:19-21).

6 Joseph believed that his circumstances were in God's hands and that things in his life had been orchestrated for both his personal well being and the survival of others. He chose to embrace the fact that God's timing is perfect. He trusted God (Genesis 50:20).

When you stop asking why things are happening and start trusting God with your circumstances, you will find that God's plan for you is always best—even when life throws tough situations your way. God has a purpose for all you face, and He will make the best of all situations, including the divorce of you parents, the loss of a close friend, and even public humiliation. Romans 8:28 promises, "We know that all things work together for the good of those who love God: those who are called according to His purpose."

 # Do What? *(15 MINUTES)*

Group Experience: Lessons from the Pit

SMALL-GROUP TIME: Use this time to help students begin to integrate the truth they've learned into their lives while they connect with other students in the group, the leaders, and with God.

Ask students to divide back into small groups and discuss the "Do What?" questions. Small-group facilitators should lead the discussions and set the model for being open and honest in responding to questions.

1. If you were Joseph, what would you have done to your brothers when they came to you for help?
   - ☐ Forgive them
   - ☐ Throw them in a pit
   - ☐ Make them serve you as your slaves
   - ☐ Have them killed
   - ☐ Make them sweat, and then forgive them
   - ☐ Nothing
   - ☐ Feed them and send them on their way
   - ☐ Other: _____

10

2. Describe a "pit" in your life that you've recently faced. How was your perspective different when you looked up from the pit? What did that situation teach you?

3. In what area do you have the most trouble when facing tough times?

☐ Blaming others

☐ Becoming bitter

☐ Questioning God's timing

4. What do you need to do in order to honor God in that area?

Small-group facilitators should reinforce the LifePoint for this session. Make sure that student's questions are invited and addressed honestly.

 # LifePoint Review

God uses everything we experience—even the most difficult circumstances—to accomplish His will and form our character for navigating the critical path

Do" Points:

These "Do" Points will help you grab hold of this week's LifePoint. Be open and honest as you answer the questions within your small group.

1. <u>Spend time with Christians whose faith has matured through adversity.</u> Many people can minister to you by sharing how God has worked in their lives.
   Share your struggles with someone who truly cares about you and can help

2. <u>Study biblical accounts of people who experienced great adversity and discovered God's will for their lives.</u> Both the Old and New Testaments are full of the stories of men and women who suffered hardship and yet still honored God.
   What can you learn from these heroes of the faith?

3. <u>Confess to God any bitterness that has resulted from trials you've experienced</u> If you can't be honest with God, you can't be honest with anyone. God knows your thoughts, good and bad.
   How can you be more honest in your conversations with God?

Prayer Connection:

This is the time to encourage, support, and pray for each other for God's help and encouragement through difficult circumstances.

Share prayer needs with the group, especially those related to hearing from and responding to God. Close the time in prayer.

Prayer Needs:

Encourage students to list prayer needs for others in their books so they can pray for one another during the week. Assign a student coordinator in each small group to gather group's requests and e-mail them to the group members.

10

now What?

Take it to the next level by completing one of these assignments this week:

Option #1:
Adopt the role of a reporter and get the scoop. Write an article as if you're reporting on an event in the life of a person from Scripture who experienced terrible circumstances, yet honored God. Consider Moses, Ruth, David, Paul, Mary, and Jesus. Or you could grab a friend and do a mock interview with one of these individuals. Record his or her character traits, the circumstances he or she experienced, and how God used the circumstances to bring about good.

Option #2:
Tape a conversation with a mature Christian who has experienced terrible hardships yet believes God used those difficulties for a specific reason. After you tape the person's story, listen again to what was said. Pray that God will develop the character traits and faith the person shows in your own life.

Bible Reference notes

Use these notes to deepen your understanding as you study the Bible on your own:

Genesis 45:4   ***I am your brother Joseph.*** Joseph's brothers were terrified of their brother whom they had sold into slavery (see Gen. 37:28). Joseph had the power to exact revenge on them because of their betrayal if he chose to do so.

Genesis 45:5   ***God sent me.*** God was working behind the scenes to carry out His purposes, namely to preserve the nation of Israel during the famine. God used Joseph as His chosen instrument in the palace of the pharaoh. God would not allow the evil actions of people to dictate his plan. Instead, we see God's sovereign control in human affairs.

Genesis 45:7   ***a remnant.*** God would not allow His chosen people, Israel, to die because of the famine.

Genesis 45:8   ***father.*** This was a title of honor given to high officials in Egypt.
lord ... ruler. Joseph's power was almost absolute; in Egypt, he was second only to pharaoh.

Genesis 50:17   ***Joseph wept.*** Joseph was both emotional and sensitive (see Gen. 42:24; 43:30; 45:2,14–15; 46:29).

Genesis 50:18   ***threw themselves down.*** This was a fulfillment of Joseph's earlier dreams (see Gen. 37:7,9).

Genesis 50:19   ***Am I in the place of God?*** Joseph wanted his brothers to know that he wasn't interested in playing God by seeking revenge on them. Joseph knew that God was the only One who could deal with injustices.

Genesis 50:20   God used the evil treatment of Joseph's brothers, being falsely accused by Potiphar's wife, and being forgotten in prison, to achieve His purpose. When we trust God during difficult times, He is faithful to work good from it.
God intended it for good. On the surface, what Joseph's brothers did to him was a terrible act. Behind the scenes, however, God was making sure Joseph was in the right position to carry out His greater plan—to save the lives of the people of Israel and the other nations who came to buy food during the famine.

10

NOTES

Session

11

LEANING ON OTHERS IN THE STORY

Connections Prep

MAIN LIFEPOINT: God places specific Christians in our lives so that we may be formed spiritually in a way that allows us to become the men and women God created us to be.

To reinforce the LifePoint, leaders and small group facilitators should understand the following more detailed CheckPoints and "Do" Points.

BIBLE STUDY CHECKPOINTS:
· Understand the importance of seeking godly counsel
· Discern those from whom you should seek counsel from those you shouldn't
· List effective questions to ask when seeking counsel

LIFE CHANGE "DO" POINTS:
· Compile a list of those whom you can trust for godly counsel
· Ask the right questions from godly counsel
· Listen for God's voice through the advice of others

PREPARATION:
☐ Review the *Leader's Book* for this session and prepare your teaching.
☐ Determine how you will subdivide students into small discussion groups.
☐ Recruit mature students or adults as small-group facilitators. Be sure these facilitators plan to attend.
☐ Print the following words on half sheets of paper: doctor, nurse, ambulance driver, preacher, theology professor, youth minister, parent, friend, principal, teacher, tutor, park ranger, Boy Scout, and grandparent.
☐ Obtain a walking stick and baseball hat.

REQUIRED SUPPLIES:
☐ *Critical Decisions: Clarity in the Journey* leader books for each group facilitator
☐ *Critical Decisions: Clarity in the Journey* student books for each student
☐ Pen or pencil for each student
☐ Signs reading: doctor, nurse, ambulance driver, preacher, theology professor, youth minister, parent, friend, principal, teacher, tutor, park ranger, Boy Scout, and grandparent
☐ A cane or walking stick
☐ A baseball hat

This "Get Ready" section is primarily for the students, but leaders and facilitators will benefit from these devotionals too.

Get Ready

Spend a few moments getting to know God. Read one of these brief passages each day, and be sure to write down anything He reveals to you

MONDAY

Read 1 Kings 12:1-4

When did you last make an agreement with someone that included a condition? What made you decide to bargain with that person?

TUESDAY

Read 1 Kings 12:5

If you knew an answer would change your life, how long would you be willing to for it? Could you wait three whole days?

WEDNESDAY

Read 1 Kings 12:6-11

From whom do you most often seek advice? Are you more likely to follow the adv of an older adult or that of a peer?

THURSDAY

Read 1 Kings 12:12-14

Describe a time when you totally disagreed with advice you received. Did you fol it, or did you make a different decision on your own?

FRIDAY

Read Proverbs 15:22

Which of your plans have succeeded? Which have failed?
What role has godly counsel played in your planning?

SATURDAY

Read Proverbs 3:7

What if you were the only person to turn to for help? Would you trust your own counsel, or would you become even more dependent on God's wisdom?

SUNDAY

Read Proverbs 12:15

How often are your decisions correct? How often do you admit, at least to yourself, that you are wrong? What is the most foolish thing you ever decided to do?

LARGE-GROUP OPENING:
everyone's attention.
ake announcements.
en your session with
a prayer. Read the
Point to the students.

Ask students to tell
out last week's "Now
What?" options. Ask
m to share what they
earned as a reporter.
t did they learn from
their interviews with
se who talked about
how God used their
ough times for good?
ime allows, you may
se to have someone
share his or her
recording.

 L i ƒ e P o i N t

God places specific Christians in our lives so that we may be formed spiritually in a way that allows us to become the men and women God created us to be.

SMALL-GROUP TIME:
Instruct students to separate into smaller groups of 4-8, preferably in a circle configuration. Call on the mature student or adult leaders you recruited to facilitate each small group through this "Say What?" segment.

Say What? *(15 MINUTES)*

Random Question of the Week:
What is your favorite breakfast cereal?

Group Experience: Whom Would You Trust?

(Permission is granted to copy only this page for use by facilitators as part of the Life Connections® Youth Clarity in the Journey study.)

Give each student one or more of the signs you made. Ask the following questions, pausing after each to allow students time to respond by raising the appropriate signs: To whom would you go if you had a medical problem? To whom would you go with a question about the Bible? To whom would you turn if you had trouble with a subject at school? Who would you consult if you wanted to learn how to build a campfire?

1. In each case, why did you choose the person you chose?

2. In what situations could you benefit from having more than one person to go to for help?

3. To whom can go for godly advice? Have you ever sought someone out for this reason?

So What? *(30 MINUTES)*

Teaching Outline

I. Everybody Needs a Little Help Sometimes
 A. Everyone is looking for counsel
 B. Many people look for counsel in the wrong places
 C. Godly counsel is the only reliable counsel

II. Learning from the Bible (Scripture)

III. Some People Intentionally Don't Seek Counsel
 A. Some people can't think of anyone to ask for help
 B. Some people are too proud to ask for help
 C. Some people don't want to hear what they already know

IV. Characteristics of Godly Counsel
 A. Reiterates biblical truth
 B. Advice would be agreed upon by other Christian counselors
 C. Options given reflect godly wisdom

Everybody Needs a Little Help Sometimes

Everybody needs a little help now and then—even if you don't like to ask for it. Parents, school counselors, and youth pastors are only some of the people you can go to for advice. ❶ There's no shame in asking for assistance, but it's important that you know whom you can trust. ❷ Television continues to devote airtime to psychics who promise to give you all needed answers in just one phone call. Newspapers and magazines continue to provide life guidance in horoscopes. Online, several happy helpers write advice columns on everything from manners to relationships—and chat rooms and blogs offer endless "guidance" on every subject under the sun.

In today's session you will learn the importance of seeking godly counsel from people who love and fear God, people who know the Bible and live according to its direction.

11

Learning from
the Bible ...

1 Kings 12:1-14

Ask for two volunteers
to come to the front
and pantomime the
parts of Rehoboam and
Jeroboam as you read
the Scripture aloud.
Ask a third student to
represent "the elders"
by using a cane. Enlist
a fourth to represent
the young men by
wearing a baseball
cap.

**LARGE-GROUP TIME
CONTINUED:**
This is the meat of the
teaching time. Remind
students to follow along
and take notes in their
Student Books.

As you share the
"So What?" information
with students, make
it your own. Use your
natural teaching style.

Emphasize underlined
information, which gives
key points, answers to
the *Student Book*
questions or fill-in-the-
blanks in the (shown in
your margins).

❸ For some people,
making decisions
causes ...

☐ **Hives**
☐ **An adrenaline rush**
☐ **Stress**

Learning from the Bible

¹ Then Rehoboam went to Shechem, for all Israel had gone to Shechem to make him
² When Jeroboam son of Nebat heard [about it], for he was still in Egypt where he ha
fled from King Solomon's presence, Jeroboam stayed in Egypt. ³ They summoned him
Jeroboam and the whole assembly of Israel came and spoke to Rehoboam: ⁴ "Your fa
made our yoke harsh. You, therefore, lighten your father's harsh service and the hea
yoke he put on us, and we will serve you."
⁵ Rehoboam replied, "Go home for three days and then return to me." So the people
left. ⁶ Then King Rehoboam consulted with the elders who had served his father Solo
when he was alive, asking, "How do you advise me to respond to these people?"
⁷ They replied, "Today if you will be a servant to these people and serve them, and if
respond to them by speaking kind words to them, they will be your servants forever.
⁸ But he rejected the advice of the elders who had advised him and consulted with th
young men who had grown up with him and served him. ⁹ He asked them, "What mes
do you advise that we send back to these people who said to me, 'Lighten the yoke y
father put on us'?"
¹⁰ Then the young men who had grown up with him told him, "This is what you should
say to these people who said to you, 'Your father made our yoke heavy, but you, mak
it lighter on us!' This is what you should tell them: 'My little finger is thicker than my
father's loins! ¹¹ Although my father burdened you with a heavy yoke, I will add to yo
yoke; my father disciplined you with whips, but I will discipline you with barbed whip
¹² So Jeroboam and all the people came to Rehoboam on the third day, as the king ha
ordered: "Return to me on the third day." ¹³ Then the king answered the people hars
He rejected the advice the elders had given him ¹⁴ and spoke to them according to t
young men's advice: "My father made your yoke heavy, but I will add to your yoke; m
father disciplined you with whips, but I will discipline you with barbed whips."

Some People Intentionally Don't Seek Counsel

What decisions are you worrying about? Chances are you have something on yo
mind that you wish would go away. You need to do something about it, but you
don't know what you should try. You recognize the need to make a decision, but
you don't know what the best decision is. In fact, you aren't even sure what you
options are.

You haven't told anyone about what you're going through, and you're beginning
feel anxious and overwhelmed. The good news is that you aren't alone. ❸ Many
people stress out over some of the decisions they have to make.

The problem is that every human has limited experience and knowledge. God has not designed us to make all decisions independently or with limited information. Unfortunately, many avoid seeking counsel from others for even the most critical decisions. This should never be the case for anyone, especially a Christ-follower.

❹ However, there are several valid reasons that you may be tempted to avoid seeking help. (1) The most obvious is that you may not be able to think of anyone who could help you. But you have parents, ministers, and mature Christian friends who would be happy to fill the void you feel. **❹** (2) Pride is another reason you may not want to admit your need for assistance. Perhaps you have come to think that you are at a point in life where others expect you to make decisions based on intuition. But one of the reasons great leaders are great is because they have learned the importance of surrounding themselves with wise people and listening to their advice. **❹** (3) It's also possible that you don't seek counsel because you already know the right answer and just don't want to hear it. One of the best things about being a believer, though, is having Christian brothers and sisters, parents, and grandparents who can help you see things from a different point of view. Their loving influence will often open your mind to God's viewpoint.

❺ Seeking godly counsel is always a good idea because sometimes you can only see things the way you want to see them. And it's also helpful when you don't have enough information to make the right decision based on your own knowledge. How true it is that "all of us are better than one of us." Other godly people can help provide the information you need to make decisions that honor God.

Characteristics of Godly Counsel

Today's Bible study presents principles that will help you make the most of godly counsel. In 1 Kings 12 Rehoboam is crowned king of Israel. During his inauguration, those assembled plead with him to cut taxes and shorten the workday. They cry out, "Your father made our yoke harsh. You, therefore, lighten your father's harsh service and the heavy yoke he put on us, and we will serve you" (v. 4). If the king had but promised to cut taxes, the people would have been pleased. But while considering the fair requests, the new king foolishly sought the advice of his friends rather than accepting the counsel of his father's older and wiser advisers.

❻ (1) How can you, unlike Rehoboam, make sure you choose wise advisors? First, determine to seek counsel from someone who will tell you the truth. You need people in your life who are more concerned with telling you what's right than with

❹ For what three **sons might you not** **seek godly advice?**

❺ Seeking godly **sel is a good idea** **for two reasons.** **ometimes you can** **see things the way** **want to see them,** **and (2) sometimes** **don't have enough** **formation to make** **e right decision on** **your own.**

❻ Check the **statements that** **describe ways to** **ose wise advisors:** **oose your best** **end**

ck someone who **lls you what you** **ant to hear**

ck someone who **lls you the truth** **matter what you** **ant to hear**

oose an adviser **ho is where you** **ant to be in life**

nd the oldest per- **n in the world**

oose more than **e person to be** **ur counselor**

oose one person **be your counselor** **d stick with them**

11

143

keeping your friendship. **❻** (2) Second, you should seek out someone whose life you'd like to emulate. Talk to an athlete if you want to be an athlete. Spend care day with a dairy farmer if you want to become one yourself. **❻** (3) Third, if poss ask more than one person for advice. Proverbs 15:22 says, "Plans fail when the no counsel, but with many advisers they succeed."

❼ Often the best counsel comes through the combined advice and wisdom of several people.

❽ Be sure to ask the right questions when seeking godly counsel. Ask things designed to help keep you on track with God's plans, such as, **❾** (1) "Are any o the options I'm considering unscriptural?" Measure all answers you receive aga what God's Word says. A good counselor will help you keep everything in the con of the Bible. And if you are new Christian, they can help you better understand the Bible says. Another important question to ask a godly counselor is, **❾** (2) " do you think is the wisest decision I can make?" Remember, every situation will have a clear answer. There may be more than one solution to a problem you are ing. But be careful: **❿** While you can expect to hear from God when seeking god counsel, you must be careful not to take everything you hear as God's word. Don pressure your mentor to speak on God's behalf. God will confirm His will for you through other people, His Word, and the promptings of His Spirit.

❼ Often the best advice comes from the combined wisdom of several ...
☐ People
☐ Friends
☐ Children
☐ Theologians

❽ Be sure to ask the right questions when seeking godly counsel.

❾ What two questions should you ask a counselor?
1. "Are any of the options I'm considering unscriptural?"
2. "What do you think is the wisest decision I can make?"

❿ True or False: You can take everything a Christian counselor tells you as God's personal word to you. (False)

SMALL-GROUP TIME:
Use this time to help
students begin to inte-
grate the truth they've
learned into their lives
as they connect with
other students in the
group, the leaders, and
with God.

Ask students to divide
back into small groups
and discuss the "Do
What?" questions.
Small-group facilitators
should lead the discus-
sions and set the model
for being open and
honest in responding to
questions.

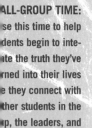  **Do What?** *(15 MINUTES)*

Group Experience: The Cost of Godly Counsel

1. What advice would you have given Rehoboam? Would you have sided with the young guys, the old men, or offered your own counsel regarding the situation?

2. In order to receive godly counsel you can depend on, what would you be willing to give?
   - ☐ An hour a week
   - ☐ Fifteen minutes every day
   - ☐ My pride
   - ☐ One weekend a year
   - ☐ $100
   - ☐ As much time as it takes
   - ☐ Other:_____

3. In each of the following areas, write one sentence describing advice you've been given:

   Friendships

   Time management

   Dealing with disappointment

   Family problems

   Study habits

   Being the best

4. What is the godliest counsel that you have received? Who or what was its source?

Small-group facilitators should reinforce the LifePoint for this session. Make sure that student's questions are invited and addressed honestly.

 # LifePoint Review

God places specific Christians in our lives so that we may be formed spiritua in a way that allows us to become the men and women God created us to be

"Do" Points:

These "Do" Points will help you grab hold of this week's LifePoint. Be open and honest as you answer the questions within your small group.

1. <u>Compile a list of people to whom you can go for godly advice.</u> There is more one person who can help you find godly answers.
   Who will be on your list of godly counselors?

2. <u>Ask the right questions from godly counsel.</u> Getting counsel requires more th just "sitting and soaking." You need to ask questions and respond to what y hear.
   Do you talk too much in a conversation? Too little? What can you do to be more responsive in a counseling situation?

3. <u>Listen for God's voice through the counsel of others.</u> God does speak through those who serve Him. He uses His Word and His Spirit to validate the words ken on His behalf.
   Will you prayerfully consider the advice you receive?

Prayer Connection:

This is the time to encourage, support, and pray for each other as you realize that God has placed people in your lives who can provide wise counsel.

Share prayer needs with the group, especially those related to hearing from and responding to God. Close the time in prayer.

Prayer Needs:

Be sure to end your session by asking ents to share prayer ls with one another, cially as they relate ssues brought up by today's session.

courage students to ist prayer needs for thers in their books so they can pray for another during the ek. Assign a student coordinator in each nall group to gather roup's requests and e-mail them to the group members.

Encourage students o dig a little deeper completing a "Now What?" assignment e the next time you et. Remind students out the short, daily Ready" Bible read- s and related ques- at the beginning of Session 12.

now What?

Take it to the next level by completing one of these assignments this week:

Option #1:

Proverbs is a book of wisdom; try to read a chapter a day. A neat thing about the book is that there's a proverb for every day of the month. This week, begin reading the chapter that matches the calendar day. For example, if you begin reading on the sixteenth of the month, then begin with Proverbs 16. Read chapter 17 the following day. Consider reading the Book of Proverbs every month throughout the year.

Option #2:

Contact three mature Christian adults from whom you would consider seeking counsel. Ask them if they would consider being a person that you can go to when you need godly advice. Set up a time to meet with each of them, and pray with them that God would use them to help you find His direction.

Bible Reference Notes

Use these notes to deepen your understanding as you study the Bible on your own:

1 Kings 12:1   ***Shechem.*** Located about 35 miles north of Jerusalem. This was a significant city in Israel's history. example, this is where the Israelites dedicated themselves to keeping the Mosaic Law (Josh. 24:1–2 After Israel divided into two kingdoms, Shechem became the capital of the northern kingdom for a period (1 Kings 12:25).

1 Kings 12:2-5   Israel wanted Jeroboam to convey their concerns over labor and taxation before Rehoboam. The pro Ahijah had already told Jeroboam that he would eventually rule 10 of the tribes after the kingdom divided. Jeroboam apparently didn't try to press the issue but, instead, let events play out naturally

1 Kings 12:6   ***the elders.*** Rehoboam sought input from those who had served as his father's official advisers. Th elders were most likely the same age as Solomon.

1 Kings 12:7   ***If today you will be a servant.*** Great leaders in God's economy are those who have a servant's hear Jesus'.

1 Kings 12:8   ***young men.*** Rehoboam assembled some of his own friends and associates for advice. Apparently, were already serving him in some official capacity.

1 Kings 12:10   ***My little finger is thicker than my father's waist.*** This hyperbole meant that the least severe treat by Rehoboam would be far greater than his father's most oppressive measures.

1 Kings 12:11   ***scorpions.*** These were leather lashes with sharp pieces of metal attached to them; it was a cruel w used during this time.

1 Kings 12:12-14   Rather than listening to the elders' advice, Rehoboam decided to serve his own interests and actua increase the burden on the people. This decision would contribute to the eventual division of the kingdom.

Session

12

THROUGH THE LABYRINTH OF LIFE

Connections Prep

MAIN LIFEPOINT: Making the critical decisions amidst life's adversities requires a wisdom unavailable by any means other than God.

To reinforce the LifePoint, leaders and small group facilitators should understand the following more detailed CheckPoints and "Do" Points.

BIBLE STUDY CHECKPOINTS:
- Explain why we need God's wisdom to handle adversity
- Acknowledge the importance of fully trusting in God
- Explain how relying on God's wisdom changes our focus

LIFE CHANGE "DO" POINTS:
- Stop trusting in worldly wisdom
- Ask God for wisdom
- Utilize the wisdom of Scripture

PREPARATION:
☐ Review the *Leader's Book* for this session and prepare your teaching.
☐ Determine how you will subdivide students into small discussion groups.
☐ Recruit mature students or adults as small-group facilitators. Be sure these facilitators plan to attend.
☐ Copy James 1:1-12 onto a piece of paper and seal it in an envelope.

REQUIRED SUPPLIES:
☐ *Critical Decisions: Clarity in the Journey* leader books for each group facilitator
☐ *Critical Decisions: Clarity in the Journey* student books for each student
☐ Pen or pencil for each student
☐ Copy James 1:1-12 onto a piece of paper and seal it in an envelope

12

Get Ready

*Spend a few moments getting to know God. Read one of these brief
passages each day, and be sure to write down anything He reveals to you.*

MONDAY

Read James 1:1-2
How does it make you feel when someone tells you to look on the bright side?
Does anyone have the right to tell you how you should feel?

TUESDAY

Read James 1:3-4
What is the first thing you do in a desperate situation? How much do you try to
endure before asking God for help?

WEDNESDAY

Read James 1:5
What is the last thing you asked God for? Do you think you have wisdom, or do you
feel you lack it? Why would anyone not ask God for wisdom?

THURSDAY

Read James 1:6
When you ask God for something, do you really believe He will give you what's be
for you? Are you ever indecisive? When you're caught between two choices, and
struggle to have confidence that God will reveal Himself to you, how do you feel
What does this say about what you really believe?

FRIDAY

Read James 1:7-8

How long does it take you to make a decision? What might cause you to fear making a decision?

SATURDAY

Read James 1:9-11

How does a delicate flower respond to the scorching summer heat? How can this be applied to our lives and the lives of others? Think about the ways you can protect yourself from the scorching heat of life.

SUNDAY

Read James 1:12

Describe a spiritual struggle you have endured. How did you feel God's hand during the struggle? In what ways did this struggle contribute to a greater understanding?

LARGE-GROUP OPENING:
veryone's attention. ke announcements. n your session with a prayer. Read the oint to the students.

sk students to share last week's "Now What?" options. Ask hem to explain how reading Proverbs ach day has helped em in making godly isions. Ask them to re about those they ntacted to serve as eir counselors. How the people react to eir inquiries? Were of the students able to meet any of their counselors?

 LifePoint

Making the critical decisions amidst life's adversities requires a wisdom unavailable by any means other than God.

12

SMALL-GROUP TIME:
Instruct students to
separate into smaller
groups of 4-8, prefer-
ably in a circle con-
figuration. Call on the
mature student or adult
leaders you recruited
to facilitate each small
group through this "Say
What?" segment.

Say What? *(15 MINUTES)*

Random Question of the Week:

Why do people refer to some shoes as tennis shoes even though they are not ma
for tennis and are rarely used for tennis?

Group Experience: Truth and Consequence

(Permission is granted to copy only this page for use by facilitators as part of t
Life Connections® Youth Clarity in the Journey study.)

Tell students to think of three true statements about themselves and one that is
false. (Ask them not to make up things that are obviously false.) If you want, yo
can ask them to complete the following sentences, making sure that one is
completed as untrue:

(1) When I was a child I _____

(2) My favorite type of music is _____

(3) My most embarrassing moment was when I _____

(4) Ten years from now I hope to _____

Ask each student to read his or her four statements aloud then let those listeni
guess which of them is false.

1. Did you identify every false statement? If not, how many did you get?

2. What method did you use to determine the three true statements from the
   false one?

3. On what do you rely or trust?

4. In the challenging times of your life, how is your reliance on God and trust in
   His wisdom evident?

RGE-GROUP TIME:
ve the students turn
to face the front for
s teaching time. Be
sure you can make
e contact with each
tudent in the room.
courage students to
low along and take
tes in their *Student
Books.*

So What? *(30 MINUTES)*

Teaching Outline

I. It's Just the Way It Is
A. Sometimes you don't know which way to turn for help

B. God loves for you to ask Him for wisdom

C. God's wisdom changes your outlook

II. Learning from the Bible (Scripture)

III. Life 101
A. Every believer experiences hardship

B. You are required to live for God

IV. Turning to God for Help
A. You need God's help to deal with life's struggles

B. God will give you wisdom to deal with life

C. God's wisdom will transform how you view life

EACHING FOR THE
LARGE GROUP:

hare the "So What?"
teaching with your
students. You may
odify it to meet your
needs. Be sure to
hlight the underlined
rmation, which gives
swers to the Student
ok questions and fill-
the-blanks (shown in
your margins).

It's Just the Way It Is
❶ There are times when you will not know what choices you should make or how to respond when the going gets tough. It's important to ask God for help. The Old Testament offers a great story about how King Solomon asked God for the wisdom to rule Israel well. Solomon knew that the job of a king was way too big for one person, and he recognized that he would have a difficult time adequately filling his role. That's why the king asked not for wealth or more power, but for wisdom to do his job. (See 1 Kings 3:9-14.) ❷ God was so pleased with Solomon's request that He not only gave him unequalled wisdom, but also unparalleled riches and honor.

❶ There are times
en you will not know
t choices you should
ke or how to respond
when the going gets
tough.

Would you dare ask God for wisdom? Most of us routinely ask for plenty yet wisdom may not be on your list of usual suspects. When you do ask God for wisdom, you can be sure He'll be pleased with your request (1 Kings 3:9). You may not receive a crown, scepter, throne, and someone to feed you grapes, but you will gain greater riches for eternity. In this session we will look at how our search for wisdom comes from the trials in life that force us to make critical decisions. We will also look at how we can ask God for wisdom.

❷ What was God's
sponse to Solomon's
request for wisdom?

12

Learning from
the Bible ...

James 1:1-12

Copy the following
Scripture onto a piece
of paper and then seal
it in an envelope. Read
the Scripture aloud to
students as if you have
just received a letter.

LARGE-GROUP TIME
CONTINUED:
This is the meat of the
teaching time. Remind
students to follow along
and take notes in their
Student Books.

As you share the
"So What?" information
with students, make
it your own. Use your
natural teaching style.
You may modify it with
your own perspec-
tives and teaching
needs. Emphasize the
underlined information,
which gives key points,
answers to the *Student
Book* questions or fill-in-
the-blanks in the (shown
in your margins).

❸ True of False: Every
believer experiences
hardship. (True)

❹ You may not be
required to forfeit your
life for God, but as
a Christian you are
required to live your life
for Him.

Learning from the Bible

¹ *James, a slave of God and of the Lord Jesus Christ:*
To the 12 tribes in the Dispersion.
Greetings.

² *Consider it a great joy, my brothers, whenever you experience various trials, ³ know*
that the testing of your faith produces endurance. ⁴ But endurance must do its compl
work, so that you may be mature and complete, lacking nothing.
⁵ *Now if any of you lacks wisdom, he should ask God, who gives to all generously and*
without criticizing, and it will be given to him. ⁶ But let him ask in faith without doubt-
ing. For the doubter is like the surging sea, driven and tossed by the wind. ⁷ That pers
should not expect to receive anything from the Lord. ⁸ An indecisive man is unstable
all his ways.
⁹ *The brother of humble circumstances should boast in his exaltation; ¹⁰ but the one w*
is rich [should boast] in his humiliation, because he will pass away like a flower of th
field. ¹¹ For the sun rises with its scorching heat and dries up the grass; its flower fal
off, and its beautiful appearance is destroyed. In the same way, the rich man will with
away while pursuing his activities.
¹² *Blessed is a man who endures trials, because when he passes the test he will recei*
the crown of life that He has promised to those who love Him.

Life 101

Some things are unavoidable: death and taxes, for example. School is another
one of those "unavoidables." Do you realize that you may be in your mid-forties
before you can stop saying that you've spent half your life in school? Of course,
education's core curriculum cannot be avoided because it's designed to be a sol
foundation from which to spring into the journey of life. Similarly, when you are
transformed as a believer in Jesus Christ you "sign up" for Christian Life 101. A
new life in Christ is wonderful, yet comes with its own set of trials.

❸ Every believer experiences hardship. You are not exempt. But God knows that
through the testing of your faith you will lay a solid foundation on which to build
spiritual maturity. Jesus warned His disciples about the trouble that would come
their way (See John 16:32-33). And trouble did come as Christians were persecu
and even killed by the hostile Roman government and zealous Jews (see Acts
7:54-60). ❹ You may not be required to forfeit your life for God, but as a Christi
you are required to live your life for Him. And living for God is not always easy.

What three reasons make it necessary for you to seek God's help in dealing with life's struggles? Adversity can result in negative attitudes. 2. Trials can lead to doubt, anxiety, indecisiveness, and passivity. Trials tend to produce impatience.

Turning to God for Help

❺ There are three reasons you need God's help in dealing with life's struggles. (1) First, adversity can result in negativity. Aware of this, James wanted to change the attitudes of the disciples living in terrible times: "Consider it a great joy, my brothers, whenever you experience various trials" (v. 2). Learning to deal with tough stuff is one thing, but becoming joyful in the midst of it is something else entirely. James recognized that his fellow disciples were confused and bitter over being run out of their hometowns and being hunted down for their faith. That's why he used the word "whenever" to point out that trials will come. Like death and taxes and relationships, hard times are a fact of life for Christ followers.

You can't prepare for the unexpected, but you can determine your attitude before trials come. ❺ (2)To do that, you need God's wisdom because trials can generate all kinds of doubt, anxiety, indecisiveness, and passivity. James says that "the testing of your faith produces endurance" (v. 3). Every time your faith is tested, you have to ask yourself if God is worth trusting. And when you continue to place trust in Him despite the bad things that come your way, you increase your "endurance."

❺ (3) Naturally, trials tend to produce impatience, but that is all the more reason why you should seek God's wisdom in facing them. James encourages you to be patient through life's difficulties (v. 4). God is working in your life to do something greater than you could ever dream of doing on your own. As you wait on Him in your troubled times, He is making you more like Christ.

How can you get the wisdom to endure trials?

❻ In verses 5 through 8, James tells you how to get the wisdom you need; you should ask for it as Solomon did: "Now if any of you lacks wisdom, he should ask God, who gives to all generously and without criticizing, and it will be given to him" (v. 5) Funny how the last person we often turn to is God. He will "generously" give to you.

When God does give you the wisdom you request, be ready to act on it. Your trust in God should not depend on the circumstances, so you should not delay in trusting Him. James has much to say on this: "But let him ask in faith without doubting. For the doubter is like the surging sea, driven and tossed by the wind. That person should not expect to receive anything from the Lord. An indecisive man is unstable in all his ways" (vv. 6-8). ❼ When you act on God's wisdom, you move from doubt to faith.

❼ **When you act on God's wisdom, you move from doubt to faith.**

12

❽ What two things will happen when you begin to rely on God's wisdom?
1.
2.

❽ <u>Two things will happen when you begin to rely on God's wisdom. (1)Your focu will move from material things to spiritual things.</u> Instead of seeing dead ends a limitations, you will see the new ways God is opening to you and the ultimate po bilities of serving Him in all circumstances. <u>(2)And you will begin to view things eternal instead of temporary.</u> Godly patience gives you the ability to see beyond y life on earth. With your focus on an eternity in heaven, you will be able to confron your circumstances with a stronger faith in God's generous wisdom.

SMALL-GROUP TIME:
Use this time to help students begin to integrate the truth they've learned into their lives while they connect with the other students in the group, the leaders, and with God.

After presenting the teaching material, ask students to divide back into small groups and discuss the "Do What?" questions. Small group facilitators should lead the discussions and set they tone by being open and honest in responding to each question.

Do What? *(15 MINUTES)*

Group Experience: Wisdom Please

1. Which of the following most tests your faith?
   ☐ Friends
   ☐ School
   ☐ Parents
   ☐ Personal weaknesses
   ☐ Job
   ☐ Your health
   ☐ Other: _____

2. What is your usual attitude toward the bad things that come your way? Are you pretty optimistic or terribly pessimistic? Does your attitude tend to rub off on others?

3. What are you going through right now in which you really need God's wisdom?

 # LifePoint Review

Making the critical decisions amidst life's adversities requires a wisdom unavailable by any means other than God.

"Do" Points:

These "Do" Points will help you grab hold of this week's LifePoint. Be open and honest as you answer the questions within your small group.

1. <u>Stop trusting in worldly wisdom.</u> Anything the world has to offer will be temporary and will always fall short of God's best for you.
   Why do you sometimes look to talk show hosts, un-Christian friends, and magazines for answers?

2. <u>Ask God for wisdom.</u> God truly does love it when you ask Him for something—especially something like wisdom.
   How easy is it for you to ask God for things? Why don't you ask Him more than you do?

3. <u>Utilize Scripture's wisdom.</u> From the Bible's first page to its last, you will find words to live by.
   What verses have you memorized that provide wisdom for dealing with tough times?

12

Be sure to end your session by asking students to share prayer needs with one another, especially as they relate to issues brought up by today's session.

Encourage students to list prayer needs for others in their books so they can pray for one another during the week. Assign a student coordinator in each small group to gather the group's requests and e-mail them to the group members.

Prayer Connection:

This is the time to encourage, support, and pray for each other as you trust in G wisdom to guide you individually and as a group.

Share prayer needs with the group, especially those related to hearing from and responding to God. Close your time in prayer.

Prayer Needs:

Encourage students to dig a little deeper by completing a "Now What?" assignment before the next time you meet. Remind students about the "Get Ready" short daily Bible readings and related questions at the beginning of Session 13.

now What?

Take it to the next level by completing this Now What? assignment:

List things in life that give you trouble. Use the space given below. What are the greatest hardships you face? Put a mark beside the ones for which you believe God has already provided you the wisdom to handle. Circle the things for which you need to seek God's wisdom. Spend time this week asking God to help you get victory over the difficulties facing you.

12

Bible Reference Notes

Use these notes to deepen your understanding as you study the Bible on your own:

James 1:1
James. "James" is probably the half-brother of Jesus who was known in the early church as "James the Just."
a servant. Here he identifies Jesus as the "Lord" (master), therefore the appropriate relationship of others to Jesus is as servants (literally "slaves").
the twelve tribes. In the New Testament, this came to be associated with the Christian church. Christians saw themselves as the new Israel (Rom. 4; 9:24–26; Phil. 3:3; 1 Peter 2:9–10).
scattered. The word is, literally, diaspora and was used by the Jews to refer to those of their number living outside of Israel in the Gentile world. Here it probably refers to those Jewish Christians living outside Israel (see 1 Peter 1:1).

James 1:2
Consider it pure joy. The joy James is talking about is not just a feeling. It is an active acceptance of adversity.
trials of many kinds. The word "trials" has the dual sense of "adversity" (e.g., disease, persecution, tragedy) and "temptations" (e.g., lust, greed, trust in wealth).

James 1:3
perseverance. Or "endurance." It is used in the sense of active overcoming, rather than passive acceptance.

James 1:4
finish its work. Perfection is not automatic—it takes time and effort.
mature and complete. What James has in mind here is wholeness of character.
lacking. The opposite of mature and complete. This is a word used of an army that has been defeated a person who has failed to reach a certain standard.

James 1:5
wisdom. This is not just abstract knowledge, but God-given insight that leads to right living.

James 1:6
James now contrasts the readiness on God's part to give (v. 5) with the hesitation on people's part to ask (v. 6). Both here and in James 4:3, unanswered prayer is connected to the quality of the asking, to the unwillingness of God to give.
believe. To be one in mind about God's ability to answer prayer.

James 1:8
double-minded. To doubt is to be in two minds—to believe and to disbelieve.

James 1:9
The brother in humble circumstances. This refers to those who are poor in a material and social se and who are looked down on by others because they are poor.
take pride. This becomes possible when the poor see beyond immediate circumstances to their new position as children of God.
high position. In the early church, the poor gained a new sense of self-respect.

James 1:10
rich. The peril of riches is that people come to trust in wealth as a source of security.
low position. Jewish culture considered wealth to be a sign of God's favor. Here, as elsewhere (vv. 2, James reverses conventional "wisdom."

James 1:11
scorching heat. The hot, southeast desert wind (the *sirocco*) sweeps into Israel in the spring "like a blast of hot air when an oven door is opened."
fade away. Wealth gives an uncertain security, since it is apt to be swept away as abruptly as desert flowers (Isa. 40:6–8).

James 1:12
Blessed. Happy is the person who has withstood all the trials to the end.
stood the test. Such a person is like metal that has been purged by fire and is purified of all foreign substances.
crown of life. Crowns were worn at weddings and feasts (and so signify joy); they were also given to winner of an athletic competition (and so signify victory); and were worn by royalty (as befits children God the King).

NOTES

NOTES

Session

13

GROWING THROUGH ADVERSITY

Connections Prep

MAIN LIFEPOINT: When your relationship with God is truly top priority, it is evident in how you decide to invest your time.

To reinforce the LifePoint, leaders and small group facilitators should understand the following more detailed CheckPoints and "Do" Points.

BIBLE STUDY CHECKPOINTS:
- Explain how to invest your time wisely
- Examine three ways we mismanage our time
- Understand how making the most of each day contributes to making decisions that honor God

LIFE CHANGE "DO" POINTS:
- Write a personal mission statement that reflects God's priorities
- Pray during your personal planning process
- Obey God by doing what He has already led you to do

PREPARATION:
- ☐ Review the *Leader's Book* for this session and prepare your teaching.
- ☐ Determine how you will subdivide students into small discussion groups.
- ☐ Recruit mature students or adults as small-group facilitators. Be sure these facilitators plan to attend.
- ☐ To celebrate the completion of the study, provide a pie or cookie cake that can be divided to feed the class.
- ☐ Supply a pie server.
- ☐ Supply a fork and a napkin for each student.
- ☐ Supply a candle and match.

REQUIRED SUPPLIES:
- ☐ *Critical Decisions: Clarity in the Journey* leader books for each group facilitator
- ☐ *Critical Decisions: Clarity in the Journey* student books for each student
- ☐ Pen or pencil for each student
- ☐ One pie or cookie cake to be divided among the students
- ☐ One pie server
- ☐ One large plate, and forks and napkins for everyone
- ☐ Candle
- ☐ Match or lighter

13

This "Get Ready" section is primarily for the students, but leaders and facilitators will benefit from these devotionals too.

Get Ready

Spend a few moments getting to know God. Read one of these brief passages each day, and be sure to write down anything He reveals to you.

MONDAY

Read James 4:13-14

Do you dream about what you will do next week, next year, or ten years from now? Are you living in the present or in the future? What might result from putting too much of your energy into what might happen down the road?

TUESDAY

Read James 4:15

Why is it important to include God into your planning? In planning the future, what assumptions are you counting on?

WEDNESDAY

Read James 4:16

In what ways could our planning be arrogant? In what ways could we be accused being boastful as we proclaim our visions?

THURSDAY

Read James 4:17

Have you ever missed an opportunity to do something good? Were you disappoint when you realized you'd missed it, or did you never intend to take the opportunity the first place?

FRIDAY

Read Ephesians 5:15

How consistent are you in your relationship with the Lord? Would someone be able to easily recognize you as a Christian?

SATURDAY

Read Ephesians 5:16

Do you enjoy each day to the fullest? If you knew Jesus was coming back tomorrow, how would you spend this afternoon?

SUNDAY

Read Ephesians 5:17

What's the most foolish thing you could do in one day?
What keeps you from doing it?

LARGE-GROUP OPENING:
everyone's attention. ake announcements. en your session with a prayer. Read the °oint to the students.

Ask students to talk ut last week's "Now What?" options. Ask m to share how God supplied wisdom for things that troubled them during the past ek. Have they called check on how their study partners are doing?

 LifePoiNt

When your relationship with God is truly top priority, it is evident in how you decide to invest your time.

13

 # Say What? *(15 MINUTES)*

Random Question of the Week:
Starfish can regrow missing arms. Why can't people?

Group Experience: Which Piece Do You Want?
(Permission is granted to copy only this page for use by facilitators as part of th Life Connections® Youth Clarity in the Journey study.)

Ask for three volunteers, and have them come forward. Place the pie or cookie c you brought on a table in front of them. Hand the first student the pie server an plate. Tell the students to imagine that the pie or cookie cake is the face of a cl representing the 12 "free hours" of a typical Saturday. Agree as a group that ei hours each day are spent sleeping and another two are spent eating, grooming, dressing, and wasting time. Ask the first student how many hours a day he or s spends doing things for him or herself. Ask the student to cut out a representati section from the cookie or pie and move it to a plate. Ask the second student ho many hours a day he or she spends doing things with or for others. Have the stu dent cut out a representative section and move it to a plate. Ask everyone to loc the remaining "hours" of pie or cookie cake. Then ask the third student to remo the amount of pie or cookie cake he or she thinks might represent the time an a age Christ-follower spends with God.

1. What do you spend most of your time doing?

2. If you could add four more hours to your day, how would you spend them?

3. How much of your day is spent learning about God's plan for you, talking to G or doing something for Him?

So What? *(30 MINUTES)*

Teaching Outline

I. The Clock Is Ticking
    A. The clock can be your friend or your enemy
    B. "Working the clock" is an important skill
    C. Nehemiah made the most of his time, not allowing himself to get distracted from his task

II. Learning from the Bible (Scripture)

III. Managing Your Time
    A. All of us have 24 hours each day
    B. Jesus has an eternal perspective on time
    C. Once time on earth is gone, it's gone

IV. Mismanaging Your Time
    A. Don't forget to include God in your planning
    B. Don't assume your future plans are set in stone
    C. Don't put off until tomorrow what you can do for God today

The Clock Is Ticking

If you ever watch reality TV, you've probably seen contestants trying to beat the clock in order to win a round of a game or to earn a more secure position among the group. In some instances, they may have to hold their breath under water for a certain amount of time. If they are really unfortunate, they may have only so much time in which to eat things you would normally call an exterminator to handle. Depending on what side you are on, the clock can be your friend or your enemy. That's why managing time becomes such a challenge and such a critical skill.

❶ "Working the clock" is important. Your ability to stay focused and make the most of the time God has given you reflects your desire to stay focused on His purpose for you. No one knew this better than Nehemiah, an interesting Old Testament figure.

13

2 What was one thing that made Nehemiah a great man of God?

As you read the following Scripture, light a candle. When you read, "For you are a bit of smoke," blow it out, and let it continue to smoke.

Learning from the Bible ...

James 4:13-17

As you share the "So What?" information with students, make it your own. Use your natural teaching style.

Emphasize underlined information which gives key points and answers to the *Student Book* questions or fill-in-the-blanks (shown in your margins).

LARGE-GROUP TIME CONTINUED: This is the meat of the teaching time. Remind students to follow along and take notes in their *Student Books*.

3 What one thing does everyone have in common?

Nehemiah provides a great example of how important it is to eliminate distractions and avoid time-wasters. His passion was to rebuild the walls around Jerusalem to bring honor to God and restoration to His people. Yet Nehemiah's mission was full of distractions. For one, some who were not in favor of his efforts asked him to stop for a while and meet with them, though they wanted nothing more than to get him off track (See Nehemiah 6:1-4.). **2** <u>Nehemiah knew he could not let anything or anyone take him from the task God had given him. For Nehemiah, fulfilling God's mission was top priority.</u> He was committed to using his time wisely.

Do you ever find yourself mismanaging the time God has given you to accomplish great things? Maybe God has called you to build a great wall. Maybe He has called you to break down great barriers. Whatever the mission, it's important to note that when distractions come, you can claim Nehemiah's motto as your own: "I am doing a great work and cannot come down" (Neh. 6:3).

Learning from the Bible

13 Come now, you who say, "Today or tomorrow we will travel to such and such a city and spend a year there and do business and make a profit." 14 You don't even know what tomorrow will bring—what your life will be! For you are a bit of smoke that appears for a little while, then vanishes.
15 Instead, you should say, "If the Lord wills, we will live and do this or that." 16 But as it is, you boast in your arrogance. All such boasting is evil. 17 So, for the person who knows to do good and doesn't do it, it is a sin.

Managing Your Time
James 4:13-17 addresses the silliness of thoughtless planning: "Come now, you who say, 'Today or tomorrow we will travel to such and such a city and spend a year there and do business and make a profit.' You don't even know what tomorrow will bring—what your life will be! For you are a bit of smoke that appears for a little while, then vanishes" (vv. 13-14). His point is that there are no guarantees in life; therefore, it makes sense to use each moment to its full potential—especially since we are to use our time for God.

3 <u>You have the same 24 hours a day that everyone else does. The difference is that only you can choose what to do with your time.</u> And what you spend your time doing is a good indicator of what is most important to you. Some people choose to waste their time by taking it for granted; others spend it on their own selfish

❹ According to the [passage], what is the wisest investment of time?

❺ Which of the following resources cannot be replaced?
☐ Water
☐ Electricity
☐ Time
☐ Solar power
☐ Gasoline

List three ways you can mismanage time:
1. Poor planning
2. Planning your future without God
3. Putting off until tomorrow what you can do for God today

What is the problem with waiting to do something for God?

desires. ❹ The Bible tells us the seek the kingdom of God and God's righteousness before anything else. Time is best spent doing those things that allow God to be realized in our lives.

One way God equips you to do this is by giving you the precious resource of time. Today you may not feel like time is a big deal, but as you grow older, that will change. In the meantime, you are wise to recognize that ❺ time is the only resource you cannot replace once it's gone.

Mismanaging Your Time

❻ (1) Poor planning is one of the most common ways to mismanage time. Think about it: how often do you fail to include an important item when you pack? How much energy is wasted worrying about the assignment that was forgotten in a rush? James says, "Come now, you who say, 'Today or tomorrow we will travel to such and such a city and spend a year there and do business and make a profit.'" The businessperson James refers to in this passage thought he had life planned down to the minute; the problem was that he forgot to pack God. James rebukes such shortsightedness in spiritual things: "You should say, "If the Lord wills, we will live and do this or that" (v. 15).

You make plans all the time: where will you go?; what will you do?; with whom will you go? But while you are planning your days and even your long term future, ❻ (2) be careful not to squeeze God out of your plans. Instead, ask Him to help you make plans. James suggests you should desire to do the things God wants that are according to His will. After all, "A man's heart plans his way, but the LORD determines his steps" (Prov. 16:9). When you include God in your planning, you remain open when God wants to rearrange your plans for His purposes.

James' businessman assumed his future plans were secure, that things would happen just as he expected. But James warns that this attitude is not of God. There is nothing wrong with planning for the future. However, you must realize that there are no guarantees in life. Your time is in God's hands, and only He knows if you'll live another day or eighty years. ❻ (3) That's why you must take care not to put off the good that God wants you to do right now. Remember, "For the person who knows to do good and doesn't do it, it is a sin" (James 4:17).

❼ Most everyone is guilty of putting things off. You'll clean your room one day. You'll share your faith with Josh one day. But the Bible is clear that when you do something you shouldn't or don't do something you should, it is sin. In Ephesians 5:15-16 Paul warns: "Pay careful attention ... making the most of the time, because the days are evil." Make the most of every opportunity—God expects it.

13

SMALL-GROUP TIME:
Use this time to help students begin to integrate the truth they've learned into their lives while they connect with the other students in the group, the leaders, and with God.

After presenting the teaching material, ask students to divide back into small groups and discuss the "Do What?" questions. Small group facilitators should lead the discussions and set they tone by being open and honest in responding to each question.

Do What? *(15 MINUTES)*

Group Experience: Can I see your ID, please?

1. Which of the following plans do you tend to leave God out of?

☐ Planning your calendar

☐ Picking the places where you will go

☐ Planning your future

☐ Doing the things you always do

☐ Deciding how to spend your money

☐ Other: _____

2. What would you like people to say about you at your funeral?

3. What are you are putting off until later, though you know God wants you to do it now? What adjustments will you need to make in order to do what God has called you to do?

 # LifePoint Review

When your relationship with God is truly top priority, it is evident in how you decide to invest your time.

"Do" Points:

These "Do" Points will help you grab hold of this week's LifePoint.
Be open and honest as you answer the questions within your small group.

1. <u>Write a personal mission statement that reflects God's priorities.</u> Write it in broad terms that reflect God's purposes for your life and how you will accomplish them.
   Have you ever written a personal mission statement? If so, how will this mission statement differ from those written previously?

2. <u>Pray during your personal planning process.</u> Sit down and plan your week, including your daily schedule, classes, practices, and special appointments.
   How can you honor God through this week's activities?

3. <u>Obey God by doing what He has led you to do.</u> God is always at work in your life. He is always calling you to serve Him in some new and exciting way.
   What did God last ask of you? Have you obeyed Him?

 13

Be sure to end your session with prayer for each other. Ask students to share prayer needs with one another and encourage them to record the requests in their books.

Encourage students to list prayer needs for others in their books so they can pray for one another during the week. Assign a student coordinator in each small group to gather the group's requests and e-mail them to the group members.

Prayer Connection:

This is the time to encourage, support, and pray for each other as continue to develop a deeper understanding of God's mysterious, complex character.

Share your prayer needs with the group, especially any related to facing the futu Your group facilitator will close your time in prayer.

Prayer Needs:

Encourage students to dig a little deeper completing a "Now What?" assignment.

now What?

Take it to the next level by completing one of these assignments this week:

Option #1:

Post a weekly calendar in your locker or room. On every day of the week, include a plan—no matter how simple it might seem—to do something specific for God. Before attempting to carry out any of those plans, make sure you are trying to accomplish the things God wants you to do rather those you choose for yourself.

Option #2:

Make a poster with the heading, "The Most." As you meditate on God's Word this week, list on the poster all the ways you can make the most of each day for God. Search Scripture for ideas and include your own.

13

Bible Reference notes

Use these notes to deepen your understanding as you study the Bible on your own:

James 4:13
Boasting about the future is arrogant because God is the only one who knows what will happen in the future.

Today or tomorrow we will go. In trade, a person in the first century had to plan ahead. Travel plan market projections, time frames, and profit forecasts are the stuff of business in all ages. Every hor merchant would plan in exactly the same way—pagan, Jew, or Christian—and that is exactly the p lem James has with these plans: There is absolutely nothing about their desires for the future, their of money, or their way of doing business that is any different from the rest of the world.

carry on business. The word James uses here is from the Greek word emporos, from which the Engli word "emporium" comes. It denotes wholesale merchants who traveled from city to city, buying and ing.

James 4:14
tomorrow. All such planning presupposes that tomorrow will unfold like any other day, when, in fac future is anything but secure (see Prov. 27:1).

What is your life? Is not death the great unknown? Who can know when death will come? By thinkin the worldly plane, the Christian business people James addressed have gained a false sense of secu

They need to look death in the face and realize their lack of control over life.

mist. Hosea 13:3 says, "Therefore they will be like the morning mist, like the early dew that disappe like chaff swirling from a threshing floor, like smoke escaping through a window."

James 4:15
If it is the Lord's will. The uncertainty of the future ought not to be a terror to the Christian. Instead ought to force an awareness of how dependent a person is upon God, and thus move that person to planning structure that involves God.

we will live and do this or that. James is not ruling out planning. He says plan, but keep God in mir

James 4:16
boast. The problem with this boasting is that they are claiming to have the future under control whe fact, it is God who holds time in His hands.

brag. This word originally described an itinerant quack who touted "cures" that did not work. It cam mean claiming to be able to do something that you could not do.

Acknowledgments:

We sincerely appreciate the great team of people that worked to develop this study on *Crit Decisions: Clarity in the Journey, Youth Edition.* Special thanks are extended to David Benr for adapting the adult study. We also appreciate the editorial and production team that co sisted of Brian Daniel, Brian Marschall, Joe Moore of Powell Creative, Bethany McShurley, Jenna Anderson.

NOTES

13

GROUP DIRECTORY

PASS THIS DIRECTORY AROUND AND HAVE YOUR GROUP
MEMBERS FILL IN THEIR NAMES AND PHONE NUMBERS.

NAME	PHONE	E-MAIL